COMBAT AIRCRAFT

152

U-2 'DRAGON LADY' UNITS 1955–90

SERIES EDITOR TONY HOLMES

152

COMBAT AIRCRAFT

Peter E Davies

U-2 'DRAGON LADY' UNITS 1955–90

OSPREY
PUBLISHING

OSPREY PUBLISHING
Bloomsbury Publishing Plc
Kemp House, Chawley Park, Cumnor Hill, Oxford OX2 9PH, UK
29 Earlsfort Terrace, Dublin 2, Ireland
1385 Broadway, 5th Floor, New York, NY 10018, USA
E-mail: info@ospreypublishing.com
www.ospreypublishing.com

OSPREY is a trademark of Osprey Publishing Ltd

First published in Great Britain in 2024

A catalogue record for this book is available from the British Library.

ISBN; PB 9781472861689; eBook 9781472861702; ePDF 9781472861719;
XML 9781472861696

24 25 26 27 28   10 9 8 7 6 5 4 3 2 1

Edited by Tony Holmes
Cover Artwork by Gareth Hector
Aircraft Profiles by Jim Laurier
Index by Alison Worthington
Originated by PDQ Digital Media Solutions, UK
Printed and bound in India by Replika Press Private Ltd

Osprey Publishing supports the Woodland Trust, the UK's leading woodland
conservation charity.

To find out more about our authors and books visit **www.ospreypublishing.com**.
Here you will find extracts, author interviews, details of forthcoming events and
the option to sign up for our newsletter.

Acknowledgements
The contributions of the following individuals were greatly appreciated –
Col Mason Gaines USAF, MSgt James C Goodall USAF, Maj Steve Randle USAF,
Terry Panopalis and Maj Bob Uebelacker USAF.

Front Cover
On 10 July 1956, CIA pilot Glen Dunaway used an early U-2A to undertake a Project *Aquatone* intelligence gathering flight over the Soviet bloc. Designated Mission 2023, it was the longest flight in a week of missions generated from Wiesbaden, West Germany, by top secret 'Det A'. The aircraft took off in darkness at 0331Z hrs and reached an altitude of 68,000 ft over East Germany, Poland, Ukraine and the Black Sea, before crossing Hungary, Rumania and Czechoslovakia. After 8 hrs 35 min, Dunaway, serving in the same unit as Francis Gary Powers, arrived back at Wiesbaden at 1206Z hrs following a 2042-mile mission. His U-2A was unmarked, apart from the spurious yellow 'NACA 163' tailband that was supposed to indicate that Dunaway's mount was a harmless weather research aircraft (*Cover Artwork by Gareth Hector*)

Previous Pages
At least seven U-2As can be seen on the ramp in this busy photograph of 'The Ranch'. An eighth aircraft is in the landing pattern over Groom Dry Lake (*CIA/Lockheed Martin*)

CONTENTS

CHAPTER ONE

BALD EAGLE AND *AQUATONE*

The U-2 proposal originated in November 1953 as Project *Bald Eagle,* a CIA initiative for a new reconnaissance type which the initially sceptical USAF would eventually buy into. It was needed to fly over the Soviet Union and provide information that was severely lacking on its military and industrial resources. The intended payload was a 500-lb camera package and radar, infrared (IR) or other intelligence gathering systems which were being developed. Eventually, the aircraft would carry five types of cameras and more than 20 electronic intelligence (ELINT) gathering and self-protection devices. It had to fly at Mach 0.8 for around 2400 miles, maintaining altitudes of 65,000–70,000 ft over 'denied territory', where the aircraft would be relatively safe from interception until around 1960, when it was estimated that adequate Soviet defences would have evolved.

The project was lent urgency by 1952 reports of Soviet long-range missile development. Concerns about the vulnerability of US bomber bases had been increased in 1953–54 by a supposedly large force of new long-range jet bombers such as the Myasishchev M-4 'Bison'. These threats were beyond the reach of US Air Force (USAF) aerial reconnaissance assets. Meanwhile, various piston-engined bomber conversions and a reconnaissance version of America's first jet bomber, the RB-45C (flown by American and British pilots) had patrolled around, and sometimes over, Soviet territory since the 1940s, but at increasingly vulnerable altitudes below 40,000 ft.

This U-2A has a fictitious NACA serial for CIA pilot training at 'The Ranch'. Early aircraft were all hand-made, so obtaining standard 'spares' was difficult. All were slightly different, which meant panels were not interchangeable. Experienced pilots claimed that the aircraft also had individual handling idiosyncrasies (*Lockheed*)

Several smaller companies including the Bell Aircraft Corporation, Fairchild Engine and Airplane Corporation and the Glenn L Martin Company were asked by the USAF to submit proposals for a better high-altitude design for *Bald Eagle*. Martin's Model 294 (a big-winged B-57 bomber) was adopted as an interim measure, while Bell's twin-engined X-16 was given a development contract. However, when John H Carter at Lockheed became aware of the project in the autumn of 1953, he suggested to company Vice-President L Eugene Root that it should submit an unsolicited *Bald Eagle* proposal. Carter felt that the high performance goals (set against the relatively low power of the available engines) would mean that weight saving – eliminating items such as a conventional undercarriage and an ejection seat – would be a major priority.

Carter also pointed out that if the aircraft's survivability extended only to 1960, unusually rapid development was essential. Following management approval, Lockheed's chief designer, Clarence 'Kelly' Johnson, started work on the CL-282 (U-2) early in 1954. His legacy of radical, innovative designs included the P-38 Lightning, P-80 Shooting Star and Constellation. He also had a reputation for completing design projects in unusually short timescales. Johnson suggested using the fuselage of his current supersonic, lightweight F-104 Starfighter design and adding 'wings like a tent' in place of the F-104's stubby, supersonic wings. The Starfighter's elongated, cylindrical fuselage and small cockpit was adapted, and a General Electric (GE) J73-GE-3 turbojet fitted in place of the fighter's GE J79. Its sideways-hinging cockpit canopy remained in all early U-2s, using the same part number as the F-104's.

The long, high aspect ratio wings were attached with three large bolts per side, like a glider's, to enable easy disassembly for air transportation. They were also early examples of the 'wet wing', with each one containing two fuel compartments holding 1335 gallons in place of conventional tanks, feeding a single sump tank.

Spanning 70 ft compared with the Bell X-16's 115 ft, the wing included glider-style 'gust control', with deployment of the flaps and ailerons to set a nose-high angle of attack that reduced stress on the wings. The Starfighter's distinctive 'high-T' tail was replaced by a lower-mounted version on a detachable tail unit. The structure was stressed to 2.5g – less than half the normal military standard. While this saved considerable weight, it made the airframe more vulnerable to aerodynamic stress than a normal design. Johnson eliminated an undercarriage, relying on two skids for landing and a wheeled dolly for take-off.

He calculated that the 13,768-lb CL-282 would exceed the specified 70,000 ft altitude limit by 3000 ft. Its tactical radius of 1200 miles gave seven hours of endurance. Johnson implied that the aircraft could be available within a year, and he expected a short production run with a limited lifespan, pending the arrival of a faster, higher-flying reconnaissance vehicle.

At first, the USAF's Wright Air Development Center (WADC) favoured the safety element of the Bell and Martin designs. Gen Curtis LeMay, who led Strategic Air Command (SAC), rejected the CL-282, seeing it as a Central Intelligence Agency (CIA) threat to his command's reconnaissance hegemony. WADC also rejected the CL-282 in June 1954, citing the lack of an undercarriage and the choice of the rare J73 over the proven Pratt & Whitney J57 engine. Fortunately, Trevor Gardner, Special Assistant for Research and Development to the Secretary to the Air Force, supported Johnson's project.

With encouragement from colleagues Frederick Ayer and Garrison Norton, Gardner took the CL-282 to Philip Strong, the CIA's Chief of Operations Staff in the Office of Scientific Intelligence. Strong in turn approached Richard M Bissell, the CIA's new Director of Planning and Coordination, who displayed interest, and Allen Dulles, CIA director, who was resistant to technological rather than traditional methods of intelligence gathering. He regarded overflights of the USSR as 'Air Force business', but President Dwight D Eisenhower insisted that it had to be a 'civilian operation'.

Also championing the high-altitude reconnaissance cause was a group of Boston scientists. Edwin H Land, founder of the Polaroid company, astronomer and optics expert Jim Baker and aeronautical engineer Allen Donovan offered their expertise in camera design and expressed their concerns about the lack of reconnaissance capability through the 'Land Panel'. Commissioned by President Eisenhower (prompted by Gardner), the panel included other distinguished academics, and it increasingly favoured Kelly Johnson's project. Johnson met the Land Panel and senior USAF figures in November 1954 and agreed to use the J57 engine and reconsider the 'skid' undercarriage.

On 24 November Eisenhower approved the CL-282 design and the Land Panel's suggestion that the aircraft should be flown by the CIA, not the USAF. Project supervision was given to Bissell by Dulles, with the comment that it was 'too secret for him to explain'. Bissell was loaned a packet of classified CL-282 documents, while Johnson began a redesign that would result in a larger airframe stressed to 2.5g (like a transport aircraft) and inevitable delays for his original eight-month period up to first flight.

Johnson learned that Pratt & Whitney could make a shorter, lighter, high-altitude J57-P-31A with its thrust increased to 11,200 lbs. Landing skids were replaced by a glider-style single main landing gear and a small metal and Teflon tail wheel. Two sprung steel 'pogo' legs with small wheels dropped away from the wings after take-off. Wingtips were protected from runway contact by abradable titanium skid buttons, lasting for around 100 landings. The large flying control surfaces were not boosted, causing work for the pilot but saving weight by omitting hydraulic systems. The wing structure used three spars and aluminium tubing lattice webs.

Normal aviation fuel tended to evaporate through the fuel tank vents at high altitude due to low air pressure. Shell Oil produced a special low vapour pressure type of kerosene, based on products used for Flit fly-spray, known as LF-1A ('lighter fuel' to the pilots). It was replaced in USAF service by the 'thermodynamically stable' JP-TS.

High-altitude flight also required a pressure suit to protect the pilot, whose blood would start to boil at 65,000 ft without cockpit pressurisation. Rather than inflict an inflated pressure suit on the pilot for an entire flight in an unpressurised cockpit, Lockheed pressurised the latter to an equivalent of 25,000–30,000 ft. The David Clark Company was asked to produce a suit that could be used uninflated for a 12-hour flight. If cockpit pressurisation was lost, the MC-3 partial pressure suit would inflate and protect the pilot for up to four hours. Each pilot had to visit the manufacturer at Worcester, Massachusetts, to be personally fitted. An ejection seat was eventually installed, but several failures occurred. The first successful ejection was not made until Col Jack Nole narrowly escaped from U-2 56-6694 when it suffered control failure at 53,000 ft on 26 September 1957.

The prototype U-2A was completed on 15 July 1955. Lockheed test pilot Tony LeVier was scheduled to make the first flight, but a suitably remote test ground had to be found as the aircraft had been designed and built at Lockheed's 'Skunk Works' in absolute secrecy. Eventually, a disused World War 2 airfield was found in a nuclear weapons test range near Groom Dry Lake, 100 miles from Las Vegas, Nevada. Officially known as Watertown Strip, but christened 'The Ranch' or 'Paradise Ranch' (according to Kelly Johnson, in deference to the primitive nature of the base), the 6000-ft runway was served by a few new buildings but initially lacked water or power.

The completed aircraft, CIA Article 341, was disassembled and flown to 'The Ranch' in a C-124 Globemaster II. Reassembled and ground tested, the 'Angel' (Johnson's preferred name for it) began taxi trials on 1 August 1955, when LeVier found that its considerable wing lift made the aircraft take off unexpectedly at 70 knots, even though he had cut the power. It flew for around 1500 ft and then LeVier had to manage the first landing, which involved a heavy bounce and a long skid that blew the main-gear tyres and burned the brakes.

The first scheduled flight, with an interim J57-P-37 engine, on 4 August was a successful 20-minute workout of the basic handling until the landing. Following Johnson's advice to touch down on the main gear, LeVier, under the CIA pseudonym 'Anthony Evans', found that the 'Angel', reluctant to stop flying, started a porpoising motion, forcing him to abort the landing. After several similar experiences he noticed an incoming thunderstorm and touched down in a stall, tail-first. With slight modification, this technique enabled U-2 pilots to return safely for decades to come.

Pilots had to master the trick of stalling the aircraft just before making contact, with guidance from another 'mobile' pilot sat in a chase car (in 1957, a supercharged Ford station wagon) travelling close behind at speeds in excess of 100 mph. He called out the last few feet of altitude to a pilot, who had only peripheral vision of the runway, communicating via an ARC-34 UHF receiver/transmitter.

Despite oil leaks, fuel-feed and flameout problems with the interim engine, the test programme showed that the prototype could meet all the specifications. Bell's X-16 was cancelled and 19 'Articles' were ordered for the CIA, together with 30 for SAC after LeMay had accepted the value of 'spy flights' in planning routes and identifying targets for his bombers. To reinforce secrecy, the aircraft became the 'Utility-2' or U-2, suggesting something as harmless as the Cessna U-3 light training aeroplane. The CIA procurement process used the cryptogram Project *Aquatone*, whereas the USAF's U-2 project was coded *Oilstone* from 3 August 1955, although many senior personnel, including Maj Gen Albert G Boyd, director of the WADC (the USAF's main research and procurement advisors) were still unaware of the U-2 programme's existence.

EYES IN THE SKIES

The U-2 project relied very much upon its cameras' ability to provide pin-sharp images from an altitude of 70,000 ft. The standard early 1950s aerial camera system could resolve images of around 25 ft in size from 33,000 ft – less than half the U-2's planned surveillance altitude. Resolution four times better would be needed, so cameras were developed in a secret project code-named NEPHO, which officially covered 'the study of clouds'.

A U-2's pressurised 'service bay' (or Q-bay) could accommodate several camera configurations and types. It was accessed from above and below. Different lower hatch covers allowed appropriate windows for each camera configuration. The A-3 configuration, common in U-2As, used three vertically mounted 24-inch focal length HR-732 cameras in a standard trimetrogon mapping arrangement. A single HR-732 and an RC-10 mapping camera comprised the A-4 fit, used for combined narrow and wider area coverage.

A massive 36-inch twin-frame, nine-position camera comprised the prototype-only C configuration. The little-used D configuration had a very long focus six-inch format camera that was vulnerable to vibration. A 70 mm Perkin Elmer tracking camera (later fitted with Mk II hand controls) recorded the U-2's progress, taking vertical views every 32 seconds throughout the flight so that the photo interpreters (PIs) could relate the main cameras' images to the aircraft's flightpath.

The widely-used, CIA-sponsored HR-73B Type B configuration camera installation photographed from vertical, near vertical and low and high oblique (showing part of the horizon) angles on either side. Projecting downwards and to the rear, the camera focused through a downward-looking prism that rapidly rotated left and right to acquire images through the row of seven rounded windows in the Q-bay belly door. These 'portholes' were protected from water splashes on wet runways by an aluminium cover, jettisoned with the pogos on take-off and re-attached after landing.

The prism's sequence gave a vertical view, with every fifth and tenth shots showing the horizon. Priority was given to vertical or near-vertical photographs. The cameras had a dual drive, and the whole module was mounted on its Image Motion Compensation platform in the laboratory before being trucked out to the U-2 and winched into the Q-bay. Air conditioning and pressurisation were provided, and the cameras were temperature-controlled to avoid distortion.

The Type B's two 300-lb canisters held two miles of Kodak thin-base Mylar film that was fed in opposite directions, one feeding forwards and the other one aft to preserve the U-2's centre of gravity at altitude. Eastman Kodak developed Mylar film base as a much lighter and stronger replacement for previous versions, using improved emulsions.

OPPOSITE
USAF camera technicians load a Type B camera into the Q-bay of a U-2A. The camera was uploaded from the bottom of the open Q-bay via a lift fixture that hooked into the upper hatch attachment points (*USAF*)

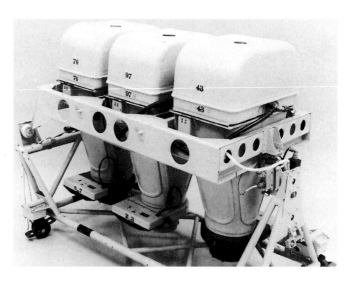

The A-3 high-resolution camera system, common in U-2As, on its transport trolley. Three vertically mounted HR-732 cameras, each with 24-inch focal length, could be operated singly or together. Each camera held enough film for 1200 9 x 18-inch exposures (*NASA/Terry Panopalis Collection*)

Exposed negatives from the two 9.5-inch-wide film strips were laid side-by-side so that each image was a useable 19 x 19-inch presentation for the PIs to examine in fine detail as they sat one each side of a Richards light table. Often, they would have to peer at 4000 images from each can, having accustomed themselves to the Type B camera's unorthodox way of simultaneously exposing two images on two film rolls. A slight gap between the images from the left and right sides of the camera operation amounted to a strip of around 600 ft of terrain in the 125 miles-wide strip normally viewed beneath the U-2's flightpath. This was due to minor overlapping of the two film rolls as they moved across the camera's focal plane.

After initial inspection for obvious revelations, the images were sent back to the USA for analysis. The image quality was unprecedented, and it enlarged easily. To show off the resolution, a U-2C was flown over the course at the Burning Tree Club in Bethesda, Maryland, at 70,000 ft, and film it exposed showed President Eisenhower's golf ball on the putting green. PIs preferred to view the negatives with lupe magnifiers for optimum detail as they peered at the stereoscopic images, fluorescently backlit, for many hours per shift.

After 1960, three Hycon HR-329 Type H cameras were introduced for use in the U-2R. With a 48-inch focal length, they could produce long-range images from more than 100 miles away. Like the Type B configuration, the Type H cameras obtained images from seven oblique and vertical angles, but the U-2 had to fly straight and level throughout a photo run.

The bulky HR 73B Type B camera installation weighed more than 400 lbs. Hycon, with Perkin Elmer, produced the hand-built Type B cameras that gave high-definition horizon-to-horizon coverage (73.5 degrees left and right), with a weight-saving single 36-inch focal length lens and shutter designed by Dr James Baker. The pilot started the camera by selecting MODE 1 on a switch in the cockpit (*Terry Panopalis Collection*)

In 1963, an Itek adaptation of the 24-inch focal length camera for the KH-4 Corona satellite became available for the U-2 as the Delta II and lighter Delta III twin-camera stereo installations. An important innovation was the Itek KA-80A IRIS II optical bar panoramic camera, using a combined mirror and lens assembly that constantly rotated, giving an unprecedented 140-degree scan angle. A film capacity of 10,500 ft and excellent resolution over a 65 miles-wide flightpath made it invaluable for extended coverage. The

KA-80A IRIS II replaced the Delta II/III and Type B cameras in the U-2R from 1969.

A lightweight ELINT package was designed by Ramo-Wooldridge to fit inside the nose and monitor Soviet C-, S- and X-band radars. It was the first of many evolving ELINT and self-protection units for the U-2.

TRAINING

The CIA had made many covert flights over denied territory, sometimes using foreign nationals as pilots so that the USA could deny involvement, but insufficient foreign pilots were available for U-2 training. Gen LeMay tasked Col Bill Yancey, SAC's former Chief of Reconnaissance, with the training of 25 SAC fighter pilots to fly the CIA's U-2 missions and a further 15 for a USAF U-2 squadron at 'The Ranch'. The first batch was assisted by several 'Skunk Works' test pilots, but the programme initially relied on only two U-2As. A C-54 Skymaster shuttled personnel to 'The Ranch' from March AFB, California, in great secrecy until it crashed on 17 November 1955, killing 14 key project officials.

Extensive medical tests were central to pilot selection and training as they signed up for well-paid, two-year CIA contracts that specified the strictest security rules. Four 'non-attributable' Greek pilots joined, but they were quickly 'washed out'. Pilots learned to 'pre-breathe' pure oxygen for up to two hours before a flight to rid their blood of nitrogen and thus avoid 'the bends'. A substantial proportion dropped out when they experienced the claustrophobic U-2 cockpit and imagined spending more than ten hours there. Others failed to cope with the aircraft's unique landing technique requirements or the punishing pre-acceptance medical assessments. The final number of qualified 'Deuce Drivers' was ten to 15 per cent of the original applicants.

By January 1956, the CIA trainees had been reduced to six, who then resigned their USAF commissions and were 'sheep dipped', becoming civilian 'test pilots' for Lockheed as a security cover. A training programme evolved, including three high-altitude flights in a T-33 Shooting Star to practise engine restarts (a consequence of the behaviour of the early J57-P-37, especially if the aircraft was poorly trimmed) followed by 'semi-stall' landings. A would-be U-2 pilot's first flight in the aircraft involved five practice landings, and the third flight was a three-hour high-altitude sortie in which the pressure suit was first worn.

Pilots subsequently gained experience of long-range navigation by day and night, camera operation and more landing practice after eight-hour flights. Early U-2 pilots each had a 'navigator' for their mission who had prepared strips of film for them that featured all of the initial points (IPs) and targets for the impending flight. The pilot could view the strips by turning a roller inside a wooden box that scrolled the film as he progressed. The navigator accompanied the pilot to his aircraft and then debriefed him after the mission.

The U-2 conversion course typically saw pilots accumulate 66 flying hours, with considerably more time spent in ground school. An important skill to absorb was accurate trimming of the aircraft to ensure it was aligned correctly with its flightpath. As the pilots learned, so did the manufacturers, refining the aircraft's fuel system, navigation equipment and radios. When the definitive J57-P-31s began to arrive in January 1956, they too needed ongoing developmental work to improve re-starting at altitude. Maintainers also had a steep learning curve. In the absence of instruction manuals, they had to rely on manufacturers' blueprints and advice from the Lockheed 'tech reps'.

At first there was only one serious mishap when Carmine Vito landed 56-6675 in gusty conditions and the undercarriage collapsed. Repaired, this aircraft became the prototype U-2C in 1959, and it suffered two more landing accidents before its career ended in a crash while Robert 'Deke' Hall was practising aerial refuelling in it as a U-2F in 1966. Jake Kratt made the first landing at a base away from 'The Ranch' after a series of flameouts that occurred more than 900 miles away. He was forced to land at Albuquerque, in New Mexico, after gliding for 300 miles. Once on the ground, his U-2 was immediately surrounded by the USAF's Air Police.

Gusting winds accounted for Maj Robert 'Pinky' Primrose's U-2 56-6703 when it crashed in September 1964 at Davis-Monthan AFB, Arizona, when he turned too steeply and stalled short of the runway after sudden crosswinds made him overshoot his turn to final approach. The programme's first fatality had occurred some eight years earlier, on 15 May 1956. Shortly after taking off in 56-6678, CIA pilot Wilburn 'Billy' Rose had found that one of the 25-lb pogo legs had failed to release from the 'gripper' fingers that held it in its socket. Turning back to try and shake the leg loose, he over-banked the U-2 and it side-slipped into the ground.

Until 1973, all training on the demanding U-2 had to be done using the early single-seat U-2A/C models. Urgent demands for a two-seater had been voiced frequently, but a series of accidents, including the death of Capt John Cunney in a heavy landing following a stall, finally forced a decision. Many of the crashes that destroyed half of the original U-2 batch occurred during a pilot's first flight, often because they had not mastered the skill of 'flying by the numbers' as the aircraft required, rather than relying on their experience of other types. The relatively slow spool-up time of the early J57 engine (17 seconds from idle to full power, reduced to six to nine seconds for the later J75) did not help pilots who miscalculated a touch-down.

As U-2 pilot Maj Steve Randle put it, 'the major difference between landing our aircraft and any other is in the last two to three feet above the runway. We have to stall the U-2 in the air in order to make it stay on the ground. Any other aircraft you can fly onto the runway, but ours has to be *stalled* onto the runway. If you stall from more than about three feet, there is a great possibility of incurring structural damage. If you misjudge and don't stall, the main gear will hit the runway and then, since you're not out of flying speed, the beast will bounce back into the air. If it bounces more than three to four feet, it will then stall, and risk damage. It's very critical, and that's why we have a mobile officer in a chase car calling off altitude. On the stall, the tail gear will settle onto the runway, followed rapidly by the main gear'.

The final moments of landing required energetic use of the control yoke to keep the U-2 level until it ran out of speed. Initiating a 15 degrees per second rate of roll at 200 knots required 85 lbs of force on the yoke. In the later U-2R/S versions the situation improved, but the balancing act required for landing was still a challenging aspect of each flight, as Col Mason Gaines, former 99th Expeditionary Reconnaissance Squadron commander at Beale AFB, California, explained;

'A lot of grappling occurred on the short final and into the flare as speed was bled off and the controls became less effective. Control inputs had to be put in, then immediately taken out, even before they took effect. If you rolled left to correct drift and then left the roll in place until it took hold, you would be too far left and needing to correct back to the right. You were constantly nudging the aircraft back to the centre line.

'It was not hard to perceive the aircraft tilting left or right after touchdown, so you could tell which way it was leaning, and correct accordingly. Fuel balance and winds were a big factor, and on some gusty crosswind days the wing was to do whatever it wanted to. Once it was down, the wingtip skidded, and could help you come to a stop, with appropriate amounts of opposite rudder. A technique for brake failure [or to combat "weathercocking"] was to put a wing down and hold it down to drag you to a stop. Of course, to a pilot, it was always a point of pride to come to a stop still "flying" the wings and keeping them level until the pogos could be re-installed. The mobile [pilot] could help, but for the most part the [U-2] pilot could do it.'

Having overcome the U-2's marked reluctance to descend, the pilot had to maintain a steady landing run of up to 3000 ft, for only a few U-2s had braking parachutes. 'Threshold', or 'T-speed', was calculated by a formula based on the aircraft's empty weight plus one knot for every 100 gallons of remaining fuel that gave the correct landing speed, which was usually ten knots above the stalling speed. Fuel was measured in gallons, not pounds, and the gauge showed 'fuel remaining', rather than the usual overall quantity.

A U-2A-1 'hard nose' sampler seen on 29 May 1962, with its pilot in an MC-3 partial pressure suit. For Operation *Crowflight*, these aircraft had a two-inch wide intake door in the tip of the nose that channelled particles for collection on four filter papers, rotated on a wheel (*USAF/Terry Panopalis Collection*)

Landing, in Maj Randle's opinion, was still an 'art rather than a science'. When the U-2 came to a halt, one wing would dip to the ground and the other would have to be pulled down to a level position so that the pogos could be reinserted. This required (ideally) one crew chief to jump up and grab the wing's edge, but depending on the balance of remaining fuel in the two outer wing tanks, two strapping crew chiefs might have been required. On narrow taxiways at some of the foreign operating locations (OLs) like Akrotiri, on Cyprus, only one pogo could be inserted, and several groundcrew would ride on the same wing as the 'pogo' to keep the aircraft level while taxiing.

Take-off in all U-2 models was a different matter, as Maj Bob Uebelacker explained. 'Initial take-off is pretty spectacular because thrust at sea level is a lot higher than it is at altitude. In fact, the older aircraft were even more impressive. The C-model could stand on its tail!' Take-off runs of 300 ft up to a maximum 1000 ft were common, with 160 knots at a steep angle being the target speed for most U-2 versions, and 180 knots as the 'red light' climbing speed for a U-2R.

On completion of his first solo flight, a new pilot was obliged to consume the traditional 'yard of beer' from a 36-inch glass bulb and tube. If all 48 ounces of ale were downed without pausing, his coveted U-2 Black Pin would slither down the neck from the bottom of the vessel too, ready to be worn.

USAF U-2s

After the delivery of the CIA's 20 aircraft from Lockheed's Skunk Works Building 82 at Burbank, California, the USAF allocation for its 4080th Strategic Reconnaissance Wing (SRW) were delivered from a different factory – a converted potato warehouse at Oildale, California, known as 'Unit 80'. They were assembled using Burbank-made parts from spring 1956 through to the end of 1957.

Airlifted to 'The Ranch' from September 1956, the aircraft were used to train pilots in Project *Dragon Lady* – a name derived from the seductive lady spy from the popular 'Terry and the Pirates' cartoon. The 4080th's first batch of pilots, trained at either March AFB or 'The Ranch', came from SAC's recently disbanded F-84F Thunderstreak strategic fighter squadrons. Their long-range navigation experience as single-seater pilots was valuable for U-2 flying. As previously noted, T-33s were also employed extensively in training after it was found that the aircraft could be used to simulate the 'floating' landing characteristics of the U-2 by holding it at half power a few inches above the runway.

When the Atomic Energy Commission increased the frequency of its nuclear weapons detonations during an expanded test programme on the Nevada range next to Groom Dry Lake, interrupting the 4080th SRW's training schedules, a move became inevitable. The wing (intended as a temporary unit, hence the four-digit title) had been activated at Turner AFB, Georgia, on 1 April 1956. When U-2As were received, the 4028th Strategic Reconnaissance Squadron (SRS) was activated and the wing moved to the remote Laughlin AFB near Del Rio, on the Texas–Mexico border, in the spring of 1957. Its first commanding officer was World

War 2 ace Col Hubert 'Hub' Zemke. U-2s occupied the northern ramp, and the support units for armament, electronics, field and organisational maintenance were in two hangars, including a 'Sferics' shop to maintain ELINT equipment and a 'nephography' shop to look after the

cameras. U-2 test work continued at Edwards AFB, California.

Preserving security then became harder. Two accidents in one day within the first month of operations were public evidence of the U-2's residency at Del Rio. 56-6702 crashed inverted on 28 June 1957 due to pilot error, killing 1Lt Ford Lowcock. 1Lt Leo Smith also died that same day after his autopilot failed and he was incapable of bailing out with an inflated MC-3 partial pressure suit.

Selection of U-2 'drivers' (a CIA security term) followed similar lines through to the 1990s, as Col Gaines observed. 'We had drivers from all backgrounds. I didn't see any appreciable difference between heavy [bomber/transport] drivers versus fighter pilots. The U-2 was so unlike anything any of us had flown before that you had to come into the programme with your eyes and ears open, and be ready to learn from the drivers who had experience in the aircraft.

'For the most part we came to the U-2 "running" from something – staff jobs, non-flying assignments, heavy drivers wanting a shot at single-seat flying, fighter pilots wanting to fly more and brief less, pilots passed over for promotion, etc. Plus we had the [Northrop] T-38s to fly on the side as well. We often referred to Beale as the land of broken toys, where all the screwballs came to dodge some bad assignment and stay in the cockpit.'

U-2A 56-6701 was one of the early SAC deliveries at 'The Ranch' in 1957, before joining the USAF's Air Research and Development Command Special Projects Branch at Edwards AFB and then reverting to SAC control in 1966. Upgraded into a U-2C, it was eventually retired and put on display in the SAC Museum at Offutt. 56-6701 was a rare survivor from the early U-2A/C batch, for of the 55 aircraft built, seven were shot down and 37 lost in accidents (*USAF*)

U-2C

Installing additional electronic surveillance packages with their drag-inducing antennas into the U-2A inevitably reduced its maximum altitude to around 67,000 ft, making the aircraft more vulnerable to interception. The 'Black Velvet' paint scheme, designed to reduce visibility even more than the CIA's Sea Blue scheme used on natural metal U-2As, added 80 lbs alone. Light weight had been crucial in selecting the U-2A, and early examples were capable of reaching altitudes in excess of 78,000 ft.

More weight meant more power was needed to maintain the average 75,100 ft maximum altitude. Johnson realised that the Pratt & Whitney J75-P-13, developed from the J57, would fit inside a U-2 with minor modification, and supply 17,000 lbs of thrust, rather than the 11,200 lbs of the U-2A's J57-P-31A. Installation of the new engine added 1450 lbs of weight to the aircraft, partly through revised structure such as enlarged air intakes and an improved horizontal stabiliser. However, altitude was also increased by 2000 ft, with better rates of climb, even though the U-2A's 2950 miles range was reduced by more than 500 miles and the high-altitude stall margin at around Mach 0.8 could be as little as four knots.

A steep climb on take-off was necessary to avoid exceeding the limiting speed, and with only a 400-lb fuel load for training, full power could not be used for take-off so as to avoid overstressing the airframe. Pilots found it harder to maintain stability at altitude, partly due to the 'slipper' fuel tanks added to the wings. The U-2's fragile structure was unchanged, and pilots had to accept that pulling back too hard on the control yoke could make the tail break off.

The first conversion (56-6675), redesignated U-2C, flew in May 1959, and the first two examples commenced service with Det B at Incirlik, in Turkey, on 1 August, with two more delivered to Det C at Atsugi, in Japan, in September. The other CIA U-2A survivors entered conversion, although many were also involved in subsequent modification programmes and consequent redesignations. Three had aerial refuelling systems installed as U-2Es, as did a single replacement U-2G (56-6682), becoming a U-2H. Four became U-2Gs for aircraft carrier trials. Six CIA U-2C/Es converted by Lockheed with in-flight refuelling gear in May 1961 became U-2Fs. SAC's 20 U-2As at Laughlin retained the J57 engine.

U-2C 56-6953 eventually fulfilled the longstanding demand for a two-seater. Having been badly damaged in a landing accident and fire in May 1972, it was chosen for a re-build with a second, raised cockpit that provided controls and instruments for an instructor pilot. The heavily modified aircraft, redesignated U-2CT, first flew on 13 February 1973, and it was joined in 1976 by a second example (56-6692). The two U-2CTs gave pilots, including Chinese Nationalist trainees, five flights before going solo, and they were used at Beale AFB until 1987.

Landing a U-2CT involved crossing the threshold at exactly ten feet and with a precise T-speed, or a 'go-around' would be needed. Landing patterns had to be flown to set altitudes – 1500 ft for the initial leg and 1100 ft on the downwind leg at T-speed plus 20 knots and 600 ft for the final, descending to 350 ft at 'T+10' to arrive at the ten-foot threshold height.

56-6701, after U-2C conversion, lands at Davis-Monthan. The aircraft's full-length dorsal fairing contained an aerial refuelling receptacle, HF radio and parts of the System 9 electronics. In-flight refuelling usually required a descent to 25,000 ft and extension of the airbrakes to prevent the U-2 from overrunning the tanker and getting caught in its slipstream. KC-135As had to slow to 200 knots to refuel the 'Dragon Lady' – fast for a fragile U-2. Indeed, two aircraft sustained structural failure while inflight refuelling (*Terry Panopalis Collection*)

CHAPTER TWO

SOVIET OVERFLIGHTS

Once the U-2 had completed its initial flight testing, the CIA wanted to begin Soviet overflights and establish whether the USSR really was developing a large fleet of nuclear bombers. Project *Genetrix* – an attempt to fly 516 camera-laden balloons across Soviet territory in January–February 1956 – had failed, and soured international relations. Weeks before, First Secretary (and future Premier) Nikita Khrushchev had rejected President Eisenhower's Open Skies proposal, whereby the two nations could legally overfly each other's territory. This was partly a Soviet ruse to disguise the lack of progress in producing a bomber fleet, while also preserving the myth that it existed, thereby forcing the USA to invest huge sums in defence.

Flights across the vast expanse of the USSR clearly required forward bases outside the USA, and the British Prime Minister, Sir Anthony Eden, was the first to be asked for *Aquatone* basing rights. Initially reluctant after the *Genetrix* fiasco, Eden was persuaded to allow four U-2s to be airlifted to RAF Lakenheath, in Suffolk, in May 1956, supervised by Richard Bissell and Kelly Johnson. A cover story was devised describing them as research aircraft, operated by the National Advisory Committee for Aeronautics (NACA, forerunner of NASA) to collect high-altitude atmospheric data in connection with planned jet airliner travel.

The deception extended to the detachment's designation as Weather Reconnaissance Squadron (Provisional) 1 (WRSP-1 was actually Det A

Built as a U-2A, 56-6680 was the first aircraft of its type to receive the 'black velvet' paint scheme – by which point it had become a U-2C. It is seen here after being further modified into a U-2F in 1966. 56-6680 made the only U-2 overflight of Moscow (on 5 July 1956), and it later participated in the ALSS programme from 1972. The aircraft has been part of the National Air and Space Museum collection in the Smithsonian Institution in Washington, D.C. since 1982 (*Terry Panopalis Collection*) of the Watertown Strip U-2 unit), which was manned by CIA pilots and USAF personnel. However, the U-2s had to be transferred to West Germany before their first overflight after the Soviet cruiser *Ordzhonikidze*, which brought Nikita Khrushchev and Premier Nikolai Bulganin to Britain on a goodwill visit during the April 1956 Suez Crisis, was allegedly spied upon by MI6 frogman Lt Cdr Lionel Crabb. This event led to a bitter dispute between the British and Soviet governments, and the withdrawal of permission for *Aquatone* flights.

Det A duly moved to Wiesbaden, in West Germany, with permission for Soviet overflights, and its aircraft received the more powerful, flameout-resistant J57-P-31 engines, becoming U-2Bs in the process. The first flight, by Carl K Overstreet on 20 June 1956, covered East Germany, Czechoslovakia and Poland, and the A-3 camera footage, sent to Eastman Kodak in the USA for processing, was clear and useful.

The urgent need to probe Soviet airfields and potential missile-building sites made further, longer missions vital. However, additional long-range sorties were initially made over eastern Europe, partly to assess whether the U-2s were being detected or tracked by radar. Ten days of missions over Soviet territory were approved on 3 July, and the first, made the following day by Hervey Stockman in 56-6680, took in East Germany, Poland and bomber bases near Minsk, before heading for Leningrad's shipyards. There was no doubt that the U-2 had been detected, as several MiGs were seen climbing to attempt an interception before soon falling away. Stockman pressed on, photographing the shipyards at Leningrad and other known bomber bases.

Fellow Det A pilot Carmine Vito was known as 'The Lemon Drop Kid' due to his consumption of these confections in flight. On one occasion, he accidentally sucked on his cyanide suicide capsule (the alternative to being captured) instead, but luckily resisted the temptation to bite. He boarded the same U-2, 56-6680, on 5 July for the only U-2 flight over Moscow, crossing Poland and suspected 'Bison' bomber bases in Ukraine en route. MiG-17s attempted an interception, but Vito was more concerned about the surface-to-air missiles (SAMs) which were thought to have been sited around Moscow, although the rather patchy Soviet radar coverage was oddly at its weakest there. He flew over several SAM sites as he photographed bomber factories, aircraft test centres and a missile development complex, all without any missiles being fired. Vito would eventually fly 65 CIA intelligence gathering missions.

Overstreet and Vito had been tracked by Soviet P-20 Periskop (NATO reporting name 'Bar Lock') and A-100 early warning radars, as had previous reconnaissance flights long-winged RB-57Ds and camera-equipped RF-100A 'Slick Chicks'. This was a worrying development for President Eisenhower, who had been reassured by Bissell that the U-2s would be undetected. Indeed, test flights against US early warning radars had shown great difficulty in tracking the U-2 accurately, or assessing its height and speed. Eisenhower wanted the illegal flights stopped, but the CIA persuaded him that the tracking was uncoordinated.

Two more flights proceeded on 9 July. Mission 2020 covered Riga, Vilnius, Minsk and Warsaw, while Overstreet on Mission 2021 flew over Hungary, Czechoslovakia and suspected bomber bases in Ukraine, but a camera fault reduced the amount of useable imagery. The flights triggered strong protest notes from the Kremlin about intrusions by a 'twin-engined medium bomber of the USAF', and these were received while Glen Dunaway was making a deep penetration into Crimea, accompanied by Soviet fighters thousands of feet below him.

The protests, followed by others from Soviet satellite states, combined with increasing fears of losing a U-2 over denied territory, persuaded Eisenhower to call a halt on 10 August. In future, each CIA overflight request would require his specific permission after close examination of each flight plan with senior CIA personnel. Bissell was aware of the great value of the first flights' imagery in providing deep insights into life behind the Iron Curtain, particularly in revealing the complete lack of the feared superiority in heavy bomber numbers on the nine suspected bases. He planned to fly U-2s equipped with radar deception devices from Incirlik, where Det B would be established. Entering Soviet airspace from the south would mean weaker early-warning radar cover and fewer interceptor bases.

Under pressure from Bissell and the Joint Chiefs of Staff, Eisenhower allowed a few flights over smaller Soviet bloc countries. One on 20 November 1956 was to overfly Iran and enter Soviet territory en route to Tbilisi, in Georgia, where the U-2 was to photograph the airfield at Sangachaly. Carrying the new Type B camera for one of its earliest operational tests, the aircraft suffered an electrical problem that caused pilot Francis Gary (Frank) Powers to abort the mission.

Det B also tested the System 4/5 signals intelligence (SIGINT) package in flights along the southern Soviet coast to explore its radar stations. An early AN/APQ-56 sideways-looking radar was also trialled in two U-2s of Dets' A and B for experimental radar photography.

Eisenhower curtailed overflights of Bulgaria, Yugoslavia and Albania again in December 1956 after three USAF RB-57Ds flew over Vladivostok, arousing protests from Moscow and displeasure from the White House, which had not been forewarned.

When it became clear that the Soviet overflights were being tracked by early warning radars and then by radar-guided SAMs, the CIA sought technical means to prolong the U-2's survivability. US scientists proposed various methods for reducing the aircraft's radar visibility that included applying a resonancy-absorbing 'second skin' or 'wallpaper' to its underside surfaces, or metal beads on wires looped around the airframe to cancel out the reflected radar waves.

The variety of frequency ranges used by the four main Soviet search radars defied efforts to find a single solution. However, in Project *Rainbow*, radar-absorbing wires and graphite absorbers on bamboo or fibreglass supports were attached to the prototype U-2's wing edges, tail and nose. Trials showed that these 'trapeze' additions reduced the radar cross-section slightly, but at the expense of range and maximum altitude. On a 2 April 1957 *Rainbow* test flight aircraft Article 341 sustained engine failure at 65,000 ft because the insulating effect of radar-absorbent material around the engine bay made the hydraulics overheat and reduce pressure to the fuel pump. Article 341 plunged out of control and test pilot Bob Sieker was killed in the first attempt at making an aircraft stealthy.

One U-2 was 'wired up' with radar absorbers for each CIA Det as a 'Dirty Bird' (Kelly Johnson's uncomplimentary nickname) or 'Covered Wagon'. They were flown along the Soviet border to test responses from radar units, with somewhat inconclusive but encouraging results that were enough to justify the start of Operation *Soft Touch* flights from Incirlik and Lahore, after permission for operations from the latter location was received from the president of Pakistan.

In 2000, the CIA released a partially redacted document on Project *Chalice* (formerly *Aquatone*) that showed Eisenhower's concerns over the possible loss of a U-2 over Soviet territory, and his instruction to halt such flights in July 1956. However, he approved a 23-day mission period in August 1957 when seven *Soft Touch* flights over the Soviet Union were authorised, together with two over China. The *Chalice* document was intended to provide 'guidance for the planning and conduct of project operations during the Fiscal Year [FY] 1961–62 time period', and it assessed the potential risks of these flights. Prepared on 14 March 1960, two months before Frank Powers' shootdown on the 24th, and final, flight over the USSR, it was adamant in advocating U-2 overflights, recommending 1057 missions in FY 1961 and 968 in FY 1962, of which many would be Soviet overflights. The document stated;

'At the time, the Soviet Union and its satellites denied normal access to its territory, so the need for a method to collect all kinds of intelligence became readily apparent and the requirement was of the highest priority. The rapid technological advances of the Soviet Union indicated the need for a prompt and aggressive reaction in order to obtain a capability which would satisfy the intelligence requirements.'

Noting that most of the previous U-2 overflights had been tracked by Soviet radar units, it used the reported success of three flights in avoiding detection as evidence that, with skilful routing and planning, 'there is an excellent chance that the entire mission can be completed without recognition by the air defence system'.

While a 'prompt and aggressive reaction' meant 'the utilisation of airborne platforms', specifically the U-2, the report's summary of the Soviets' threatening 'rapid technological advances' did not include a timely assessment of the S-75 Dvina (SA-2 'Guideline') SAM system that would bring U-2 flights over the USSR to an end only two months after its publication.

Soft Touch, including overflights from Incirlik and Lahore, was intended to examine distant top priority targets. The first attempt on 4 August 1957 by one of the three U-2s at Lahore, routed over Sinkiang province in China, Mongolia and Irkutsk and Ulan Ude in the USSR, was a 'weather abort'. 'Buster' Edens' mission the following day with a *Rainbow*-modified U-2 carrying the Type B camera was directed at the Kapustin Yar range near Stalingrad, where new ballistic missile types with ranges of up to 4000 miles were believed to be under test. A previous Det C mission to the area from Atsugi on 8 June had met only dense cloud, as did follow-up flights ten days later, but SIGINT data from the CIA indicated that a massive rocket (the R-7 Semyorka, given the reporting name SS-6 'Sapwood' by NATO) was being prepared at Kapustin Yar. Edens flew over territory with sporadic early-warning radar coverage and secured a distant shot of the new launchpad at Tyuratam (now called the Baikonur Cosmodrome).

Six more missions from Lahore were planned to fly directly over suspected sites of atomic research and weapons manufacturing in the Kuznetsk Basin, at Krasnoyarsk and Tomsk and other secret locations. They began on 12 August in better weather and ran for 16 days until the 28th. Two brought back excellent imagery of nuclear bomb testing sites near Semipalatinsk and a missile launch pad at Tyuratam. The final mission occurred a week after the first SS-6 launch. Weighed down with the 'Covered Wagon' attachments, the U-2 could only reach 66,000 ft, and interceptors got uncomfortably close at around 55,000 ft. During another 'Covered Wagon' sortie the aircraft involved struggled to reach 59,000 ft.

Half of the missions from Lahore went undetected by Soviet radar due to the lack of comprehensive coverage in the southern USSR, rather than radar-absorbing additions. Several missions in October 1957 had to be terminated because large numbers of interceptors shadowed and harassed them. Another 'Dirty Bird' mission from Eielson, Alaska, in September detected no missiles. On 4 October, an SS-6 was used to launch the Sputnik 1 satellite rather than a warhead, giving the USSR an enormous propaganda coup as the 'first nation in space'.

Rapid advances in Soviet defence technology in the late 1950s required increasingly extensive reconnaissance, with consequent demands on the U-2 detachments. Flights over the Mediterranean were needed to gather information on the USSR's new nuclear, missile-launching submarines. Its Northern Fleet required additional Arctic region flights to gather ELINT and photo imagery of its Murmansk base. Det A at Giebelstadt, which was its West German home following a move from Wiesbaden in October 1956, covered both the Mediterranean and Murmansk shortly before being closed down in November 1957. Its flightpaths over eastern Europe were more politically risky than those of the other detachments. Det A's assets and many of its personnel were transferred to Det B at Incirlik and Det C in Atsugi, which took on the additional surveillance tasks.

After the launch of two Sputniks in eight days in 1957, the CIA demanded further overflights of the missile launch and research complexes to assess the development of the intercontinental ballistic missile (ICBM) threat and find their launch sites. U-2s were allowed to patrol the Soviet border for SIGINT collection if a test missile launch was thought to be imminent, but overflights were not allowed until 2 March, when Tom Crull of Det C flew a U-2 over military installations in the eastern USSR. He was tracked and intercepted, but managed to escape.

After another failed 'spy balloon' effort (Project *Moby Dick*), Eisenhower reluctantly allowed U-2 flights to be made from a forward location at Bodø, in Norway, ostensibly for sampling duties. Several SIGINT missions were undertaken along the Soviet border in October 1958, although there was no opportunity to photograph the ICBM bases.

Despite the embarrassment of the 1956 Lakenheath debacle, the CIA was keen to involve Britain fully in the U-2 programme – information on *Aquatone* flights was customarily passed to British intelligence agencies. Prime Minister Harold Macmillan agreed to a group of four pilots being trained at Laughlin in April 1958 within the *Aquatone* programme, which was renamed *Chalice* the following month. One of the aviators, Sqn Ldr Chris Walker, died on 8 July 1958 when he lost control after suffering oxygen starvation at high altitude over Texas in U-2A 56-6713. Like several other pilots of the 12 U-2s that had been lost by August 1958, Walker's attempt to use his ejection seat failed. With Sqn Ldr Robbie Robertson as a replacement, the British contingent joined Det B covertly in Turkey in October 1958. RAF participation there enabled U-2 flights over areas of the Middle East that were of particular interest to Britain.

The CIA, with Richard Bissell as Deputy Director (Plans) from December 1958, placed increasing importance on U-2 activities, and on finding a suitable replacement, as well as having control of its own satellite reconnaissance programme. However, the 4080th SRW also asserted its role in monitoring Soviet defences from around 15 miles offshore. This included a series of *Congo Maiden* photo sorties from Eielson AFB by three U-2s around the Siberian coast in March 1959. Missions in March 1960 observed Soviet fighter airfields in the frozen terrain, and assessed the chances of SAC bombers avoiding Soviet radar as they entered from the north. The presence of many interceptors and ever-expanding Soviet radar coverage was noted.

SA-2s were fired at a U-2 *Congo Maiden* mission along the Siberian coast on 16 April 1960. The pilot concerned was unaware of the threat until his film recorded a SAM rising towards him, but fortunately not matching his altitude. The last *Congo Maiden* flight was made by Capt Dick Leavitt on 1 May while Frank Powers was flying the final, disastrous mission over the mainland.

The quest for ICBM launch pads continued to pre-occupy the CIA in 1959, as did Eisenhower's wish to avoid exacerbating international tensions by permitting more overflights, particularly as the Russians were threatening to close off Berlin. He remained unconvinced by CIA assurances that U-2s would not be shot down, and preferred to wait for a higher-performing successor to provide a much better safety level. Eventually, when it was known that ICBM tests at Tyuratam had been resumed, including the launching of a Luna rocket with a moon probe, the president was reminded that no U-2 overflights had occurred for 18 months. Border flights continued in the hope of using telemetry signals intelligence equipment in a U-2 or a SAC RB-47 to record the telemetry signals generated during the launch of an R-7 missile, and this was finally achieved on 9 June 1959.

By July 1959 Eisenhower eventually conceded the requirement for an overflight of Tyuratam, organised as Operation *Touchdown* and involving a U-2 mission from Peshawar, in Pakistan, which would cover the launch site, move to other priority targets in the Urals area and recover for the first time in Iran, where the Shah was still an ally. C-130s transported the support equipment via an RAF airfield in Bahrain to Peshawar, followed by Frank Powers from Incirlik in a U-2 carrying an HR-73B camera. Marty Knutson flew the first planned 'test' mission successfully, penetrating deeply into Soviet territory undetected and recovering to Zahedan, in Iran. His film revealed the Luna launch site, and another one under construction.

The CIA maintained pressure on Eisenhower for more overflights of Tyuratam, but it was limited to 14 U-2C ELINT flights around the southern Soviet border in the second half of 1959 to gather telemetry data on missile launches and attempt to film them from long distances. An overflight of the launch site was finally approved in November in Operation *High Wire*, with the mission being performed on 6 December by Det B's RAF pilot, Sqn Ldr Robinson.

In the first such operation flown by a British aviator, Robinson undertook a highly successful mission from Peshawar, through Afghanistan and over Tyuratam to photograph the extensively developed launch complexes at Kasputin Yar. Here, he found new R-12 Dvina (SS-4 'Sandal') nuclear missiles, and 37 M-4 'Bison' bombers at Saratov/Engels airfield. More than 60 Tu-95 'Bear' and Tu-16 'Badger' bombers, among other aircraft, were also photographed at Saratov/Engels, as were transport links possibly leading to other missile bases. Finally, his cameras recorded SA-2 SAM batteries defending Kapustin Yar. Robinson returned to Incirlik in 56-6684, despite the U-2C's reduced range, rather than diverting to northern Turkey, although he had to omit the Kazan bomber factory at Kuybyshev from his target list to save fuel.

A mission with British pilot Flt Lt John MacArthur occurred on 5 February 1960 as Operation *Knife Edge*. It covered no fewer than 571 locations, including the Kazan aircraft factories, airfields, industrial and military installations, ports and harbours. Bomber airfields were of particular interest to the analysts, and MacArthur's imagery showed seven probable Tu-22 'Blinder' bombers and a heavy concentration of military airfields in Crimea. However, there was still no further sign of new ICBM launch sites.

Eleven RAF pilots were ultimately trained to fly the U-2 under CIA supervision. Sqn Ldr Dick Cloke was involved in trials for the U-2R as an instructor pilot in 1969–70 and Sqn Ldr Martin Bee flew the carrier-modified U-2G.

With such productive U-2 missions still possible, and delays both in finding its successor and in developing the Corona reconnaissance satellite, it was difficult for Eisenhower to resist the pressure for additional flights. The last successful attempt, Operation *Square Deal*, was flown on 9 April 1960 from Peshawar in the hope of locating the elusive launch sites.

With Norway and Turkey ruled out as start points for political reasons (both countries avoided tensions with their Soviet neighbour), Pakistan offered the last practical base for long Soviet overflights. Missions from Peshawar also seemed to avoid Soviet early warning radar, although the radar chain across the southern borders was soon to be completed. A last-minute crew change put the CIA's Bob Ericson in the cockpit of 56-6684 rather than a British pilot. As with the previous mission, a second U-2C (56-6688) carrying only a tracking camera undertook a diversionary sortie.

The mission explored Tyuratam, as well as nuclear and missile testing grounds at Semipalatinsk at the flight's northern extreme. Repetitive search patterns were flown near Lake Balkash, inevitably giving the defences a better chance to plan a response. MiG-19 and Su-9 fighters attempted interceptions,

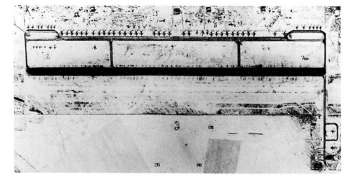

Soviet heavy bombers, photographed on Engels air base during U-2C Mission 8005 (Operation *High Wire*) from Peshawar by RAF pilot Sqn Ldr Robbie Robinson on 6 December 1959. The Type B camera imagery was often slightly blurred on purpose in development (as seen here) for released copies in order to disguise the camera's true capability (*CIA/Terry Panopalis Collection*)

and Ericson unknowingly flew above an active SA-2 site that had not installed warheads in its missiles. He managed to return safely to Zahedan, pursued for 200 miles across the border by two frustrated MiG-19 pilots who hoped to catch him descending, but ran out of fuel. By that time MiG pilots were attempting interceptions over the Black Sea, far from Soviet territory.

Ericson's imagery showed launch pad construction for the new R-16 (SS-7 'Saddler') missile and new radars for a Soviet antiballistic missile development. Khrushchev, while angry at the failure to intercept the flight, refrained from complaining, possibly adding to a sense of false security at the CIA about its planned future missions.

GRAND SLAM

Operation *Grand Slam* was planned as another penetration into the same areas of northern USSR and the industrial areas in the Urals, before surveying northwesterly rail routes and culminating in a covert landing in Norway. These long missions pushed the U-2C's range to its limits, even with very careful fuel management. They involved flying a lot of straight 'legs', rather than evasive zig-zags, easing the Soviet radar operators' task and giving SAM batteries more time to prepare their launch sequences. The mission on 1 May 1960 was the only one of four requested operations approved by Eisenhower, and it came right at the end of his final deadline on further flights imposed ahead of a summit conference in Geneva on 16 May, where Khrushchev would appear.

The threat of SA-2s, their ability to hit targets at 70,000 ft and their rapid spread around cities and into areas frequented by U-2s was, by 1960, belatedly understood by the CIA, although there were doubts about the weapon's accuracy above 60,000 ft. One of the defended cities was Sverdlovsk, which lay on the *Grand Slam* route. It was hoped that U-2 missions could continue if careful routing kept them away from known SAMs and allowed pilots to avoid early warning radars long enough to prevent SA-2 operators from setting up missile launches. High altitude was also still thought to provide some survivability.

With presidential approval, the support aircraft took fuel, supplies and crews (including Bob Ericson and Det B safety officer Frank Powers, two of the senior pilots in the U-2 programme) to Peshawar. Marty Knutson was assigned the task of returning the mission aircraft to Incirlik, and Glen Dunaway was to fly that U-2 (56-6691) on to Peshawar. Bad weather cancelled the latter flight on 28 April, and Ericson returned the U-2 to Incirlik again. That evening, the weather looked clearer, and the aircraft was brought back to Peshawar. Preparations proceeded, but in the final hours another postponement was announced, requiring Dunaway to return the U-2 to Turkey yet again. The same news was received again on 30 April, leaving only one more day for *Grand Slam*.

A better forecast on 1 May persuaded CIA chief Dulles to give the go-ahead. A different U-2 had to be used because 56-6691 had run out of hours after its stop–go return flights to Incirlik, and 56-6693, better known as Article 360 but not rated by pilots as the best U-2C, was next in line. Rebuilt after a crash-landing in Japan as a result of fuel exhaustion

in September 1959, the aircraft was regarded as a 'hangar queen' with fuel transfer problems and other odd behavioural characteristics. However, it had the J75 engine, the Type B camera and System 6 electronic countermeasures (ECM).

Ericson flew 56-6693 to Peshawar early in the morning, and he remained there as Powers' mobile pilot while John Shinn suited up as the standby pilot. Both aviators had doubts about the distances involved, and there was discussion about Powers taking the sole suicide device (hidden in a silver dollar, and replacing the poison capsule) with him.

Fuelled and equipped with a HR-73B camera and two 5000-ft rolls of nine-inch film, the unmarked black U-2 started up after delays in receiving the CIA 'go-code', and it took off at 0625 hrs, arriving over the Soviet coast 30 minutes later and appearing on their radars. Khrushchev, attending the traditional May Day military parade, ordered the U-2 to be destroyed at all costs and grounded civilian aircraft to free the skies for interceptors. Powers flew over solid cloud until he reached the Aral Sea near Tyuratam, and then visibility deteriorated again as he headed for Sverdlovsk, fighting an unreliable autopilot and encountering difficulty in navigating. His ultimate goal on the northerly flight was Murmansk and then Norway, but he only made about half that distance.

Over Tyuratam, Powers attempted to secure camera footage and avoid two SAM sites, with a third being unmanned due to the May Day holiday. Others were alerted when it was decided that the U-2 was heading towards the Urals – an area full of 'secret cities' where visibility was much better. The U-2 autopilot continued to malfunction, repeatedly causing the aeroplane to pitch up. Normally, that would have been a reason to abort the mission, but Powers struggled on, looking for clear skies. This decision, regarded by many of his colleagues as a very brave one, was later criticised by Secretary of Defence Robert S McNamara as that of a 'reckless young fighter pilot'. Powers passed more SA-2 batteries at Chelyabinsk (south of Sverdlovsk), but they did not coordinate their P-12 Yenisei ('Spoon Rest

Francis Gary 'Frank' Powers in high-visibility coveralls over his partial pressure suit. U-2R N800X (68-10331) has an SSB radio and refuelling receptacle in its dorsal fairing. The tail wheel provided steering on the ground via a cable and pulley system connected to the rudder pedals. A tow-bar known as a 'sulky' lifted the tail wheel off the ground hydraulically (*Terry Panopalis Collection*)

A') and RSNA-75 ('Fan Song') radar data. The radar circuits of one of the latter systems failed and its three screens went blank.

As Powers flew towards Sverdlovsk, waves of MiG-19 and Su-9 interceptors rose to meet him. Capt Igor Mientyukov, without a pressure suit and flying an unarmed, newly delivered Su-9, was ordered to ram the U-2. He accelerated at Mach 1.9 towards the unseen 'Dragon Lady', guided by ground control, only to overshoot and have to abandon the pursuit when Powers began a turn. Although two MiG-19s took up the chase, the U-2 was now close to the 4th Independent Army's SA-2 batteries near Sverdlovsk.

Capt Nikolai Sheludko's battery was the first to fire three SA-2s, but Powers was already beyond their range. Maj Mikhail Voronov, supervising the next SA-2/13D battery in the absence of his commander, received height, range and direction data for the target and ordered a salvo of three missiles to be fired. Only one ignited and launched, but it followed the 'Fan Song's' automatic tracking mode and headed straight for the unsuspecting Powers as he made a 90-degree turn onto his new heading at 70,500 ft. It covered the 14-mile range at Mach 2 and exploded behind the U-2. Powers was aware of a brilliant orange flash.

Some of the missile warhead's 3600 metal pellets had shredded the aircraft's tail section, part of which broke off, causing an overall structural failure of the wings and break-up of the whole airframe. The cockpit section entered a 4g inverted spin, preventing Powers, in his inflated pressure suit, from reaching his ejection handle or the cyclonite charge destruct buttons marked ARM and DESTROY for the aircraft's secret camera. He later stated that not only did he fear an ejection in that situation could have severely injured his legs, he was worried the timer that activated the Model 175-10A's cyclonite charge was going to run out before he could escape from the tumbling cockpit.

Kelly Johnson (left) with Frank Powers, who became a Lockheed test pilot in 1970 upon his return from captivity in the USSR. Project *Idealist* U-2R N803X (68-10329) is in the background (USAF)

Voronov, uncertain that the cloud now appearing on his radar was U-2 debris or electronic jamming, delayed reporting the interception, and his regiment commander ordered another battery to fire three SA-2s. Powers attempted a manual bail-out, jettisoned his canopy, activated his emergency oxygen and released his seat belt, but did not disconnect his oxygen hoses. Somehow, he was thrown clear over the nose and his parachute opened, although an iced-over helmet visor prevented him from seeing what was happening. The second salvo of SA-2s homed onto the falling debris and two exploded near it, without injuring Powers. Still unaware of the true situation, the commander of a third battery reported that he was tracking a target, and he was ordered to fire three missiles.

Sadly, the new target consisted of two MiG-19s, sent to intercept Powers but allegedly using wrongly-coded IFF transponders. Belatedly, their pilots were told to dive rapidly to avoid the oncoming SAMs, but one, Snr Lt Safronov, was hit and died in a failed ejection. The other pilot, Capt Aivazian, dived to safety.

Powers' parachute delivered him to a farmer's field, and he was soon in KGB custody in Moscow's Lubyanka Prison at the end of the last U-2 overflight of Soviet territory. He had received no preparation for this situation, on the assumption that he would simply die or use the poison coin in his pocket – Powers' interrogators quickly found it. In the unlikely event of his surviving such a high-altitude bail-out, it was assumed that there was little point in trying to withhold information since the interrogators would have ways to get it.

The recovery crew in Norway waited five hours for Powers before returning to Oslo and announcing that Article 360 was overdue. The CIA, with presidential approval, urgently rehearsed its cover story that stated the U-2 had accidentally strayed off course from a NASA weather research mission over Turkey. The pilot had sent a message saying he had oxygen problems. He had then allegedly fallen unconscious, and the U-2, on autopilot, had strayed over Soviet territory. To have any credibility, the explanation relied on the CIA's assertion that the pilot would not have survived (due to the 'silver dollar') and the U-2's camera would have self-destructed.

Meanwhile, the aircraft's wreckage was carefully collected. Its light structure meant that large parts landed with little additional damage. Film from the relatively intact cameras was processed and the classified, undamaged SIGINT systems were explored. Powers was shown the remains, and he was surprised to see official USAF placards, serial numbers and manufacturers' nameplates had been left on many of the parts.

Faced with all this evidence, Powers could not deny the purpose of his flight, but he told his interrogators little more than they could deduce from their own observations, claiming to be just the 'driver', with no knowledge of the aircraft's systems or the purpose of the flight. Shortly after Washington's cover story was released on 3 May, it became clear to the US Ambassador in Moscow that Powers had survived. This was backed up by evidence from the CIA's new 'super spy', Col Oleg Penkovsky, who emerged at the time as the most valuable source of information on Kremlin activity.

Washington's story was then modified to imply that a rogue CIA official had illegally arranged the mission. Nothing more was said about the incident until 7 May, when Khrushchev revealed the horrifying news that Powers was alive and the U-2's remains had been inspected. He displayed a photograph of a Soviet airfield, allegedly taken by Powers.

Two days later, Eisenhower, who had dreaded exactly this outcome, took upon himself full responsibility for the U-2 programme without admitting that he authorised each flight. He added that Soviet secretiveness made these flights necessary. Leaders of all the countries that had provided temporary bases also claimed ignorance of the purpose of the flights. Deniability extended to the Japanese and British governments at the cost of good relations with the USA. Khrushchev used the propaganda value of the situation to collapse the Geneva summit. Powers faced a show trial in August 1960 and was eventually released from prison in exchange for the Soviet spy Rudolf Abel (known as William Fisher) and two hapless American students in February 1962.

Powers' failure to use the 'silver dollar' or to activate the self-destruct devices was widely criticised in government, and the new CIA director, John McCone, was particularly censorious, withholding an Intelligence Star award which Powers eventually received only after McCone's departure. In 1962 Powers became a Lockheed test pilot, flying the U-2. He then flew a camera-equipped helicopter for a Los Angeles TV company and was killed in 1977 when it crashed due to fuel starvation. In 1987 Powers was belatedly, and posthumously, awarded the Distinguished Flying Cross (DFC).

Although U-2 Soviet overflights ended with the downing of 56-6693 on 1 May 1960, the intelligence gathering effort continued with offshore ELINT flights by 38th SRS RB-47H reconnaissance bombers forward-based a Brize Norton, in Oxfordshire. On 1 July 1960 one was shot down by a MiG-19 whose pilot, Capt Vasily Polyakov, acted on his own initiative on the pretext that the SAC aircraft was flying within Soviet airspace. Four of the six crew died. Rather than being punished, Polyakov was awarded a medal by Khrushchev.

Khrushchev's closure of the German border and erection of the Berlin Wall brought new fears of nuclear conflict and fresh demands for the resumption of U-2 overflights. Although it was fairly clear that the Soviet ICBM force was still no real threat, definitive information was lacking and Corona satellite imagery was not of sufficient quality to ascertain the situation – only three out of 21 Corona 'passes' had yielded useful material, often due to cloud cover. In 1961's Operation *Yellow Moon*, the 4080th SRW flew a U-2A with an A-1 camera configuration over the same track as a SAMOS satellite to compare the quality of the imagery, with results that remain unpublished.

Gen Thomas Power, LeMay's successor as SAC commander, was adamant that new overflights were needed, and President John F Kennedy came close to ordering a resumption during the 1961 Berlin Crisis. Kelly Johnson was urged to hurry the conversion of the USAF's first six U-2As into J75-powered C-models. In view of the Powers debacle, and the continued improvements in Soviet air defences, he was also asked to develop rearward-facing IR countermeasures against air-to-air missiles – this took the form of 'sugar scoop' fairing under the tailpipe to shield the U-2's own IR signature. Lockheed also built a more comprehensive self-destruct system that would blow up all sensitive equipment.

New tactics were explored for penetrating Soviet defences, including several simultaneous 4080th SRW missions. The CIA wanted at least six target areas in northern USSR surveyed, using Thule, in Greenland, as the base, but after much discussion it was decided that U-2 losses would be punitive and further planning was ended.

The Land committee, which promoted 'the Lockheed super glider', optimistically asserted that at 70,000 ft it would be 'well out of the reach of present Russian interceptors and high enough to have a good chance of avoiding detection'. At 15,000 lbs weight, unarmed and 'devoid of military usefulness, it would minimize affront to the Russians, even if through some remote mischance it were detected and identified'. U-2A 56-6715 is seen here in high-visibility markings whilst assigned to the 4080th SRW as a 'hard nose' sampler aircraft in the early 1960s (*USAF/Terry Panopalis collection*)

CHAPTER THREE

SAM RESPONSE

Nuclear-capable bombers necessitated major changes in the defensive capability of nations threatened by them. Previously, heavy attrition by fighters and anti-aircraft artillery (AAA) could eventually make bomber attacks too costly, but the realisation that one bomber in a first-strike formation could obliterate a city made the destruction of all intruding bombers vital. Devastating raids by Allied bombers in World War 2 prompted the development of German SAMs like the V2-based Wasserfall and radio-controlled Henschel Hs 117 Schmetterling, which were tested in the final stages of the conflict.

Captured information on these projects enabled Soviet scientists to begin work on similar designs post-war. Little was achieved until 1951, however, when Premier Josef Stalin, concerned at the USAF's heavy bomber attacks on North Korea, ordered the urgent development of the single-stage Almaz S-25 Berkut missile. By 1954 Berkut SAM sites had appeared near two massive ring roads, specially constructed around Moscow. Prolonged development made the Berkut obsolescent by June 1956, when it finally became fully operational. A new, cheaper and more mobile system was needed for the wider defence of Soviet territory, so the S-75 programme was begun in November 1953. It led to the two-stage SA-75 Dvina, with its RSNA-75 'Fan Song' track-while-scan command guidance radar, and the improved S-75N Desna, with a high-frequency SNR-75 radar unit. Both were primarily intended to defeat SAC B-47 Stratojet and B-52 Stratofortress bombers.

U-2A N805X was used at Edwards AFB in June 1969 to test NCR 'Magic Paint' in a series of short-lived attempts to reduce the aircraft's visibility to interceptors. The 'chameleon' stripes changed from green on the ground to other colours in lower temperatures at altitude. N805X was also given a white polka dot finish as part of the 'camouflage' trials to produce a visually confusing image (*Terry Panopalis Collection*)

Managed by the Fakel design organisation, the SA-2 entered service in December 1957, with plans for 265 missile batteries, each one including six SM-63-1 missile launchers, a 'Fan Song' guidance radar, a 'Spoon Rest' initial acquisition radar with a 125-mile range, a generator and command vehicles. A SAM regiment consisted of three batteries and a supporting technical battalion, and the former could be moved to a new area within a few hours. SA-2s were deployed around Moscow by early 1958, with other batteries defending Leningrad and Baku. The S-75N was not available until May 1959.

DVINA VERSUS 'DRAGON LADY'

Hervey Stockman's U-2, overflying the USSR on 4 July 1956, was detected at 72,000 ft (the maximum altitude of the early S-75 missile) by Soviet radar, as was Carmine Vito's cruise across Moscow. At the time there were no armed and fuelled missiles at the local sites. In response to these missions, Khrushchev ordered a more powerful 11D (SA-75M) version of the SAM that would reach 82,000 ft. Also, missiles were to be prepared at sites near anticipated 'spyplane' routes. The SA-75M was publicly displayed at a November 1957 Moscow parade as a deterrent. The new 11D was not ready until April 1958, but caution by President Eisenhower had already limited further U-2 flights and routed them away from SAM sites. Dvina's initial success would occur over China, but the target was an RB-57D reconnaissance aircraft, not a U-2.

The May 1960 loss of Powers' U-2C had far-reaching consequences for America's international relationships (which had been improving with the USSR) and, specifically, for U-2 operations. Both of the overseas detachments returned to the USA and were absorbed into Det G at Edwards AFB. Det C had only two aircraft left, and its departure was hastened by the Japanese government following sizeable demonstrations against the U-2's presence, particularly after the crash-landing of Article 360 near Atsugi. All personnel associated with Det B at Peshawar were speedily evacuated, and a coup put a new Turkish government in place that was not party to the CIA's activities at Incirlik. Three of Det B's aircraft were airlifted to the USA and a fourth was left there for several years until the facility was closed down altogether.

To add further opprobrium to the programme, the first Administrator of NASA, T Keith Glennan, decided that association with the U-2 had become damaging and the agency should 'disengage from the programme'. However, new world crises in the 1960s would soon show that the aircraft was still needed.

The May 1960 shoot-down had shown that a single SA-2 out of 15 fired on that occasion could destroy a U-2 if it detonated relatively close to the aircraft. It was also clear that high levels of training and coordination were required to operate the complex SAM system effectively, even though these qualities

The Soviet S-75 Dvina (SA-2 'Guideline') SAM was often called the U-2's nemesis. The Chinese reverse-engineered SA-2 in the form of the HQ-1 Red Flag was particularly effective against RoCAF U-2s (*István Toperczer Collection*)

were conspicuously lacking on 1 May. Soviet defenders had even enjoyed the benefit of clear skies for their radar tracking, as all other air traffic was cancelled. The CIA had underestimated Soviet radar's ability to track U-2s, and the Kremlin did not advertise this capability because it would also have drawn attention to the fact that they could not, until May 1960, shoot one down. The scarcity of protest notes from Moscow attested to that.

Like other pilots, U-2 'drivers' had only two defences against the missile. The most effective was ECM for jamming or deception, but in 1960 the relevant devices were still being developed. In their absence, a pilot could try to out-manoeuvre the missile. In a tactical aircraft at lower altitudes, that required strenuous manoeuvring that cost altitude and energy and required perfect timing. For a fragile U-2, such moves were reduced to a shallow turn in the hope that the missile's guidance fins would have insufficient air at high altitude to make the necessary directional change. For Powers and other U-2 pilots in 1958–60, neither strategy was applicable, as they had no warning of the missile's approach and no available countermeasures.

Powers' mission was flown against a background of increasing evidence that Soviet overflights were becoming too hazardous. Soviet radar had been underestimated by the CIA. Prophetic voices in the Agency had asserted that, despite faultless performances by its pilots and no mechanical failures, the U-2 could not survive beyond 1960.

The problem of security around route planning was also raised in the post-mortem on the 1 May flight. Powers, upon returning to the USA, asserted that two National Security Agency SIGINT analysts who defected to the USSR could have been forewarning Moscow of U-2 operations. He also questioned the authenticity of the delayed 'go code' transmitted to launch his flight, and raised the possibility that Pvt Lee Harvey Oswald, a US Marine Corps radar operator at Atsugi, could have deduced and passed to the Soviets information on the U-2's maximum altitude. There was no definitive evidence for any of these theories, but they did draw attention to the increasing risks of operating spy flights, particularly from forward locations.

CUBAN MISSILE CRISIS

The U-2 was vital in monitoring Khrushchev's ambitions to make Cuba a virtual Soviet state on America's doorstep. Like the final Soviet overflight, the Cuban crisis of 1961–62 showed both the weakness and success of the US intelligence network. After Fidel Castro's rebel government seized power in Cuba in 1959, political and trading relations with the USA broke down in January 1961. On the assumption that Castro could not survive long, the CIA planned an armed invasion by Cuban counter-revolutionaries – the disastrous Bay of Pigs campaign in April 1961.

Ahead of the invasion, CIA U-2s of Det G based at Laughlin AFB undertook Project *Idealist* missions from October 1960 to April 1961. The first two in Operation *Kick Off* on 26–27 October 1960 were to reconnoitre potential invasions site and assess Cuban defences. Cloud cover meant poor photographic results, so Operation *Green Eyes* included three missions in November, with better outcomes. Another 15 U-2 flights in Operations *Green Eyes*, *Long Green* and *Flip Top* were needed to prepare for the invasion, and to film its consequences (*text continues on page 44*)

1
U-2A 56-6708 of the 4080th SRW, Laughlin AFB, Texas, June 1957

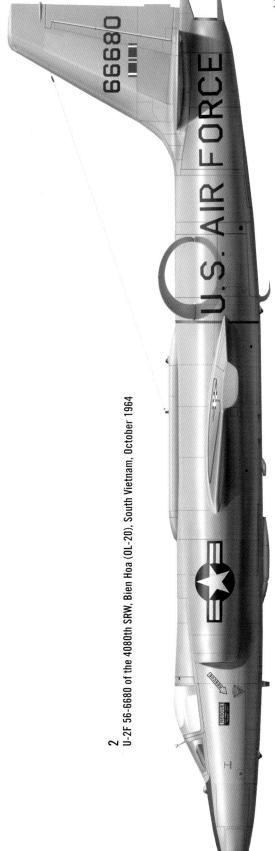

2
U-2F 56-6680 of the 4080th SRW, Bien Hoa (OL-20), South Vietnam, October 1964

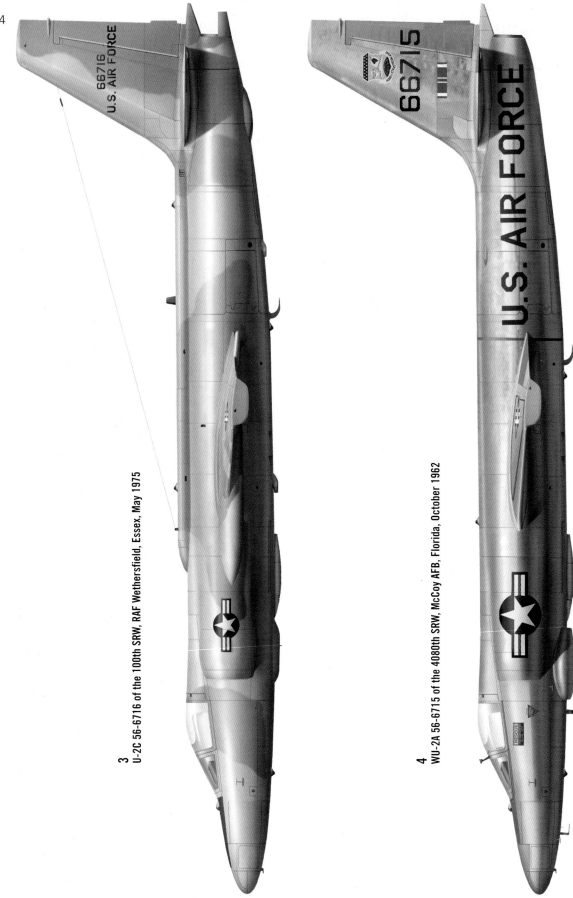

3
U-2C 56-6716 of the 100th SRW, RAF Wethersfield, Essex, May 1975

4
WU-2A 56-6715 of the 4080th SRW, McCoy AFB, Florida, October 1962

5
U-2F 56-6676 of the 4080th SRW, McCoy AFB, Florida, October 1962

6
U-2C 56-6693 of Det B, Incirlik, Turkey, 1 May 1960

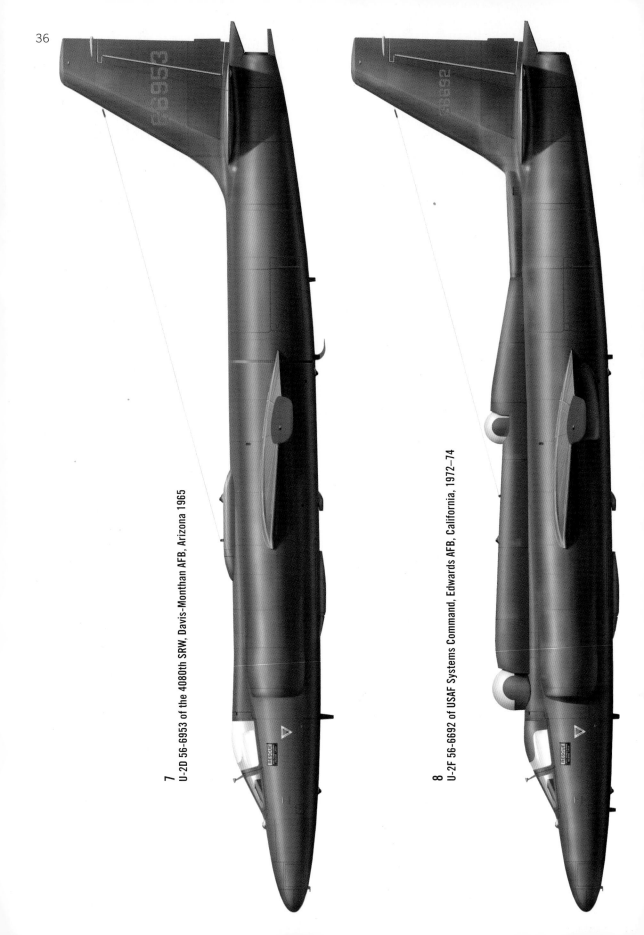

7
U-2D 56-6953 of the 4080th SRW, Davis-Monthan AFB, Arizona 1965

8
U-2F 56-6692 of USAF Systems Command, Edwards AFB, California, 1972–74

N802X

9
U-2F 56-6682/N802X of Det G, Takhli RTAFB, Thailand, 1963

3512

10
U-2C 56-6691/3512 of the 35th Squadron, RoCAF, Taoyuan AB, Taiwan, 1965

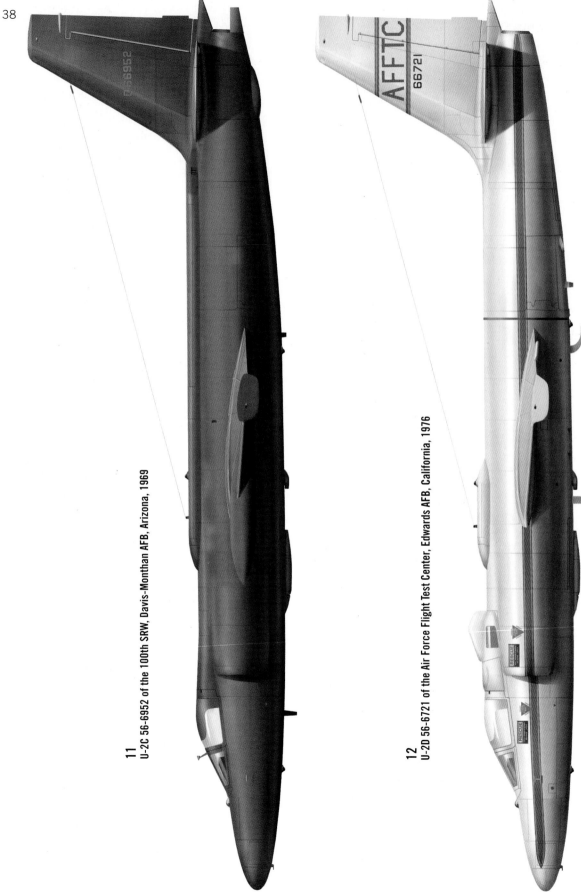

11
U-2C 56-6952 of the 100th SRW, Davis-Monthan AFB, Arizona, 1969

12
U-2D 56-6721 of the Air Force Flight Test Center, Edwards AFB, California, 1976

13
U-2R 68-10339, *Senior Lance* and EP-X trials, various locations, 1968–72

14
U-2A/D 56-6722 of the USAF Air Research and Development Command, Edwards AFB, early 1961

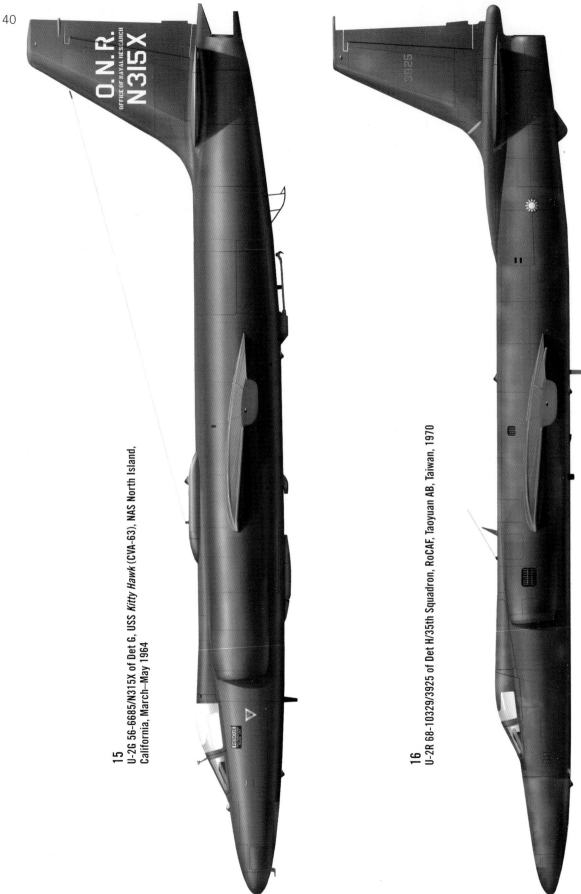

O.N.R.
OFFICE OF NAVAL RESEARCH
N315X

3925

15
U-2G 56-6685/N315X of Det G, USS *Kitty Hawk* (CVA-63), NAS North Island,
California, March–May 1964

16
U-2R 68-10329/3925 of Det H/35th Squadron, RoCAF, Taoyuan AB, Taiwan, 1970

17
U-2R 68-10331 of Det H/35th Squadron RoCAF, Taoyuan AB, Taiwan, 1971

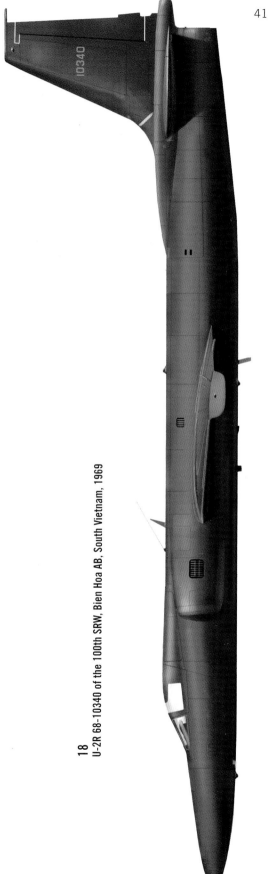

18
U-2R 68-10340 of the 100th SRW, Bien Hoa AB, South Vietnam, 1969

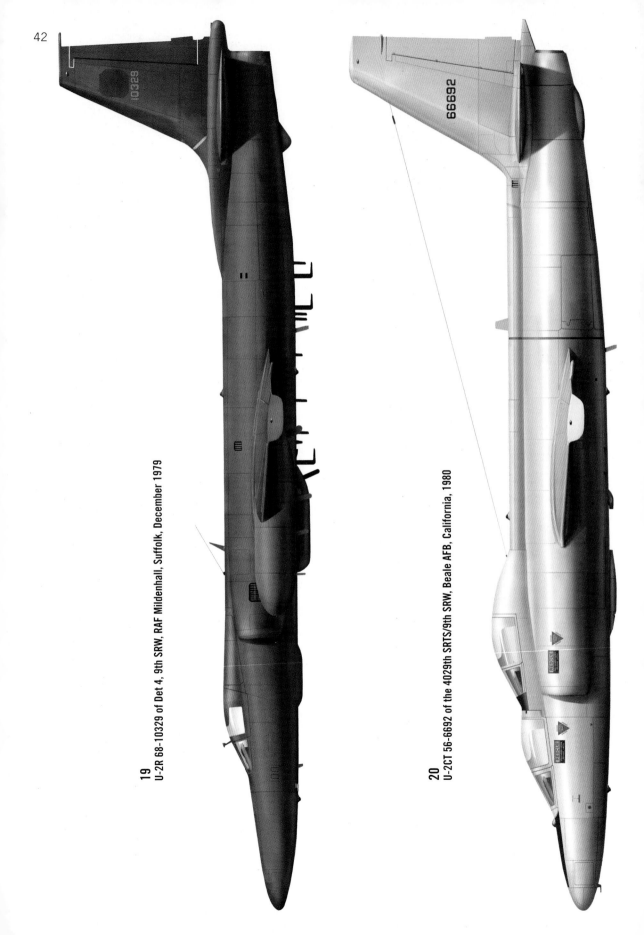

19
U-2R 68-10329 of Det 4, 9th SRW, RAF Mildenhall, Suffolk, December 1979

20
U-2CT 56-6692 of the 4029th SRTS/9th SRW, Beale AFB, California, 1980

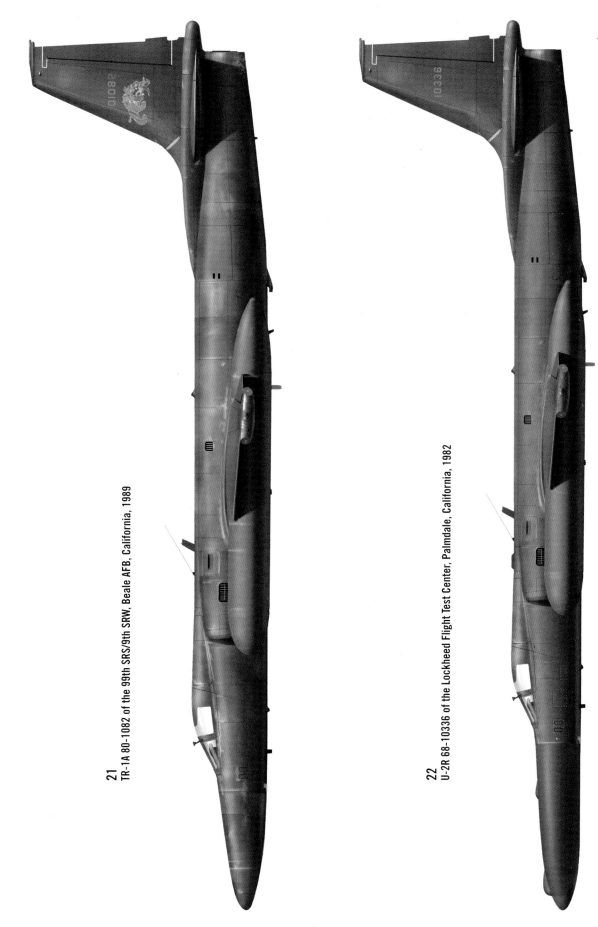

21
TR-1A 80-1082 of the 99th SRS/9th SRW, Beale AFB, California, 1989

22
U-2R 68-10336 of the Lockheed Flight Test Center, Palmdale, California, 1982

particularly post-strike imagery of the planned destruction of Castro's small air force.

The conspicuous failure of the invasion encouraged a previously disinterested Soviet regime to see opportunities for influence in support of the avowedly Marxist–Leninist Castro. Trading agreements were signed and Khrushchev foresaw means of establishing forward missile and bomber bases within reach of the USA. He regarded them as equivalent to US bases in Turkey and Italy, within ten minutes' range of the USSR. Cuban-based missiles would have a much shorter flight time than ICBMs from the USSR, and they could evade US early warning radar. Fears of another, more determined US invasion attempt made Castro very willing to accept large quantities of Soviet air defence weaponry, as well as nuclear-armed medium range ballistic missiles, SSM tactical cruise missiles, Ilyushin light bombers and MiG fighters.

Bearing a 4080th SRW patch and Distinguished Unit Citation award ribbon on its tail, U-2A 56-6715 was one of the wing's aircraft that were diverted from sampling duties for missions over Cuba from McCoy AFB. Here, groundcrew are re-attaching pogos to the wing undersides after a training flight some two years before the Cuban Missile Crisis (*NARA*)

The first wave of equipment in Operation *Anadyr*, which arrived from 26 July 1962, included the 11th Missile Air Defence Division with SA-2s, requested by Castro early in 1961, and elite MiG-21F-13 unit 32nd Guards Air Fighter Regiment. A total of 144 SA-2 launchers (originally intended for Egypt) in eight air defence regiments was the goal. By October 1962 Cuba hosted 24 SA-2 sites, 14 SS-4 'Sandal' and SS-5 'Skean' (R-14 Chusovaya) ballistic missile sites and five airfields home to MiG-17, MiG-19 and MiG-21 fighters and Il-28 'Beagle' medium bombers.

This mass of equipment and personnel had been shipped in from the USSR in great secrecy, while U-2 flights, often overflying the island for up to three hours, continued from 23 May 1961 in Project *Nimbus*. Pilots tried to complete the three-hour flight from Laughlin before 0800 hrs as clouds would build up thereafter. A rather predictable pattern of timing, course planning and flight lines over Cuba became established.

Monthly missions in 1961 were doubled in May 1962, and in June they revealed the first signs of SAM site construction, although the missiles were still in transit. At the CIA, John McCone was alone in fearing that SA-2s were intended to protect high-value medium range ballistic missile sites. However, the discovery did result in greater care over the allocation of U-2 flights over the island in a climate of opinion that now saw such overflights as provocative to the point of encouraging conflict. To some critics they were even 'illegal or immoral'. A CIA report noted that;

'In planning for any U-2 operations over well-defended denied territory, we were always aware of criticism that attended the U-2 incident over the USSR in May 1960. Also not helpful were two other incidents that served to sharpen the already existing apprehensions regarding U-2 missions.'

One involved Capt Bob Spencer's SIGINT-equipped U-2A straying over Soviet territory on 30 August 1960. Flying from Kunsan, in South Korea, he encountered turbulence and had to hand-fly the aircraft, drifting slightly off course and overflying Sakhalin Island, north of Japan, for nine minutes. MiGs were scrambled but the SA-2 batteries held their fire. The other incident resulted in Lt Col Chen Huai-Sheng's Chinese Nationalist U-2 being shot down over the Chinese mainland on 9 September 1962 by SA-2s.

Extra safety measures were arranged for U-2C/F flights, including USAF Air Rescue Service SA-16 amphibians on coastal patrol and fighters on standby in Florida and Guantanamo Bay. RB-47H SIGINT collectors patrolled distantly, monitoring SAM sites. Det G flights at first covered the whole island from west to east, but the arrival of SA-2s meant re-routing missions offshore or in brief overflights of selected areas.

By 29 August, U-2 imagery from a flight by Bob Ericson showed at least eight established and equipped SA-2 sites and Komar-class missile patrol boats. By 5 September there were 13 sites, and the first signs of the 39 MiG-21s and 20 MiG-19s delivered to Santa Clara air base in crates. McCone was concerned that nuclear-capable missiles might follow, but there was no evidence, and Khrushchev had issued a categorical assurance that there would be 'no surface-to-surface missiles or offensive weapons placed in Cuba'. The 5 September U-2 photographs had shown an anti-shipping missile system near Havana on a site which the CIA soon identified as a cruise missile installation. Understandable nervousness about flying U-2s anywhere near SA-2s meant that each mission had to be fully justified.

Several days later, the Kremlin sent its commander in Cuba a list of weapons still en route, including FKR-2 cruise missiles, Il-28 bombers and six nuclear bombs, together with permission to 'make your own decision when to use the nuclear means of [these weapons] as instruments of local warfare for the destruction of the invaders on the Cuban territory' in the event of a second invasion attempt.

U-2 reconnaissance in September was hampered by cloud cover, and by suspension of the missions after the loss of Maj Chen Huai-Sheng's 'Article', so it was not until 29 September that three more SAM sites were detected. U-2s were then instructed to take oblique images from 25 miles offshore to avoid SA-2s, with less useful results, although five more sites were detected on 5 and 7 October. It was becoming clear that the whole island was going to be defended by SAMs.

Realising that he had to 'do something about Cuba', Kennedy conceded to Gen LeMay's requests and ordered all U-2 flights to be managed by SAC from 12 October as Operation *Brass Knob*. He feared another Frank Powers situation, but the decision understandably caused resentment among CIA personnel associated with the U-2 operation. The strong feelings operated both ways, as SAC pilots believed that the Agency 'drivers' were being paid four times as much as they were. This meant that the 11 pilots of the 4080th SRW, using the CIA's three Sea Blue U-2Cs and air-refuellable U-2Fs, all with 'sugar scoop' IR tailpipe shields and SAM-warning devices in their cockpits, would carry the burden. They recovered to McCoy AFB (OL-X), Florida, where 4080th SRW commander Col John Des Portes ran the U-2 operation, bringing the total to ten available aircraft. Later in 1962, the U-2 operation was moved to Barksdale AFB (OL-19), Louisiana.

Veteran U-2 pilot Maj Steve Heyser is inserted into his MC-3 partial pressure suit for a 4080th SRW mission over Cuba in October 1962 (*USAF Terry/Panopalis Collection*)

SAM avoidance tactics were established by the wing. When his cockpit warning light, or a visual sighting of missile contrails provided enough notice, the pilot had to execute a 30-degree turn to take him out of the SA-2's range, then make an 'S' manoeuvre to get back on course. An aural warning told the pilot when a SAM was in final guidance mode. Pilots did not expect to receive warning of attempted interceptions by MiGs.

Up to five missions a day were flown, with the U-2s carrying less fuel and lighter film loads in order to reduce weight and thus maintain a 75,000-ft ceiling. Although USAF overflights of foreign territory were technically an act of war, presidential advisors were already drawing up three contingency operational plans that included tactical air strikes by 500 aircraft, amphibious assaults on the Havana area and the destruction of missile sites and MiG bases. They would all be supported by low-altitude photo-reconnaissance by US Navy and US Marine Corps RF-8A Crusaders of VFP-62 and VMCJ-2 and USAF RF-101C Voodoos from the 363rd Tactical Reconnaissance Wing in Operation *Blue Moon*.

At the same time, offshore U-2 flights were discontinued in favour of short overland surveillance of specific objectives. The first, by Maj Steve Heyser, one of the most experienced 4080th SRW pilots, in U-2F 56-6675 on 14 October changed the situation drastically. Heyser's Type B camera film, processed at the 4080th SRW's 'Recce Tech' laboratory and SAC's 544th Research Center at Offutt AFB, Nebraska, and then sent to the CIA's National Photo-Intelligence Center for interpretation, clearly showed medium-range ballistic missiles, SS-4 transporters and erectors near San Cristobal.

Workloads at the photo-processing labs subsequently increased to the point where technicians, who worked with CIA personnel peering over their shoulders, desperate for results, had to sleep in the laboratory. A single film batch took around eight hours to develop, and five copies of prints from each one had to be made, including a set for the president.

The true crisis had begun, and Kennedy, shortly to face mid-term elections, resisted advice to permit military action as the 'hawks' in government wished. However, he wanted comprehensive reconnaissance cover of Cuba, so four U-2s were despatched from Laughlin. Urgent missions on 17 October showed that the missile sites and MiGs were being uncrated and assembled rapidly. Capt Buddy Brown was among the five who flew the first surveillance mission on 17 October, taking off in appalling weather from Laughlin in a U-2A with a Type B camera and slipper tanks containing ELINT equipment.

Missions on the 19th and 20th made clear that these preparations were happening throughout the island. A MiG-21 was photographed taking off,

Maj Heyser's photographs from 'Article 342' (56-6675) during Mission 3101 on 14 October showed SS-4 missile trailers, erectors and tented accommodation in western Cuba. There were also multiple AAA sites and six SA-2 sites in that part of the islands. Project *Idealist* CIA U-2C pilots spent 459 hours photographing Cuba in 1961–62 before control of the missions passed to the USAF (*CIA/Public Domain*)

but it did not pursue the U-2. In fact, the SAM batteries and MiG units were under orders from Gen Issa Pliyev, senior Soviet commander on the island, not to engage U-2s. On 22 October these orders were modified by an ambivalent note from Moscow stating that missiles could be loaded and fired only on direct orders from the Kremlin, but also stating that Pliyev and his air defence commander, Lt Gen Stepan Grechko, should 'repulse the enemy'.

Although the missile warheads were not yet evident, it was known that each SS-4 or SS-5 would be fitted with a 3000-lb warhead of one megaton, or 80 times the power of the Hiroshima weapon. Sixteen SS-4s were already visible in western Cuba. Kennedy held on, but he received more depressing news after a 19 October U-2 flight, by then under SAC control, showed active cruise missile sites on the coast and revealed that 24 active SAM sites were in place as a real threat to reconnaissance flights. The steady build-up of Cuban 'defences' continued with the addition of 12 more Komar-class missile patrol boats and a rising total of 101 fighters.

On 22 October Kennedy announced his response – a naval blockade of Cuba. VFP-62 prepared for its first RF-8A photo missions the next day from NAS Key West, Florida, pilots from the unit wishing they could have had access to the U-2s' classified *Talent* photographs to help them navigate at low altitude and near-sonic speeds to their target sites. It was later realised that USAF pilots had received annotated copies, but misunderstandings at US Navy command level meant that the photographs were not available to RF-8A pilots for several days. With this confusion resolved, the Crusader pilots brought back detailed photos of the San Cristobal missile sites, taken with KA-45 five-inch format cameras at tree-top level and very high speed.

The heads of government of Western nations were presented with copies of the U-2 photographs and an explanatory letter from Kennedy. A further display of U-2 and RF-8A photos at the United Nations (UN) scuppered Soviet denials that any offensive weapons were installed in Cuba, decisively moving the opinion of the UN against the protestations of Soviet Ambassador Valerian Zorin.

Intense low-altitude sortie levels were maintained as SAC was placed on DEFCON-2 (the highest state of alert prior to a war footing) on 24 October, and two U-2 missions observed the MiG airfields and the missile sites. Entire Soviet military encampments were revealed and, most alarmingly, 9K52M Luna-M ('Frog-7') missiles capable of nuclear destruction over a 1300-mile range. Kennedy had to balance demands for air strikes or invasion against the knowledge he had received about the rapid increase in the threat level from Cuba. Although several U-2 missions encountered obscuring cloud conditions, more were ordered, and two pilots, Heyser and Maj Rudolph Anderson, were frequently scheduled. Pilot fatigue became a concern.

The situation was briefly complicated again by the accidental overflight of a northern section of the

President John F Kennedy (right) discusses the missile photographs taken by Maj Steve Heyser (centre) on 22 October 1962. Next to Kennedy is Gen Curtis LeMay. Col Doug Steakly, head of the Pentagon's Joint Reconnaissance Center, and Lt Col Joe O'Grady are on the left. RF-101 pilot O'Grady was awarded a DFC following a low-level reconnaissance mission over Cuba, which was subsequently featured in *TIME* magazine (*Getty Images*)

USSR by Maj Charles Maultsby, flying a 4080th SRW sampling mission using an F-2 sampling hatch, from Eielson AFB (OL-5), in Alaska, on 27 October. A 'Duck Butt' SC-54D search and rescue (SAR) aircraft orbited near Barter Island, off the Arctic coast of Alaska, in case Maultsby had to eject between there and the North Pole.

Confused by the Northern Lights and the usual problems of navigating near the North Pole, where complex 'grid' navigation was required, Maultsby took an inexact star 'fix' and found himself over Siberia, and about to run out of fuel after more than nine hours airborne. He shut the engine down, whereupon his suit inflated, his helmet faceplate and the windshield misted over and he began to descend, expecting to bail out over the Arctic wastes. He was soon out of radio range from the 'Duck Butt'. Luckily, he was heading back towards Eielson AFB, although for security reasons its radar station was unable to give him a 'steer' to keep him out of Soviet airspace.

Two nuclear missile-armed F-102A Delta Dagger fighters flown by Capts Dean Rands and Leon Schmutz were scrambled from Galena FOL, in Alaska, to escort Maultsby back to an airfield at Kotzebue radar station, also in Alaska, unaware that six MiGs had tried to intercept him earlier. Fortunately, he had turned away from Soviet territory just in time. Maultsby landed on Kotzebue's runway, covered with a foot of snow, without damage. The U-2 was flown out after a C-47 transport had delivered barrels of fuel, and its batteries had been re-charged.

Statements by Khrushchev on 26–27 October appeared to have a more conciliatory tone, suggesting the trading of Cuban missiles for those in Turkey together with assurances that the USA would not invade Cuba. Meanwhile, Castro was finding the constant low-altitude surveillance of Cuba increasingly humiliating, and he encouraged his AAA batteries to tackle the elusive fast jets more effectively.

On 27 October came the devastating news that one of the two available U-2Fs borrowed from the CIA had been shot down near Banes and its pilot, Maj Rudy Anderson, had not escaped. Anderson, chief of Flight Standardisation, had rivalled Heyser over the number of Cuba missions he had flown, and he volunteered for an extra one on the 27th, covering a secondary target. He had been Mobile Control Officer for a mission by Capt Chuck Kern that was scrubbed at the last minute. The normal practice was that the 'Mobile' pilot would then get the mission when it was re-scheduled. Capt Brown was assigned the primary target in western Cuba on 27 October, but it was weathered out, so Anderson was called in for his secondary target on the fourth U-2 mission of the day.

He took off at 0909 hrs for a diagonal pass across Cuba, turning to fly past Guantanamo Bay and an area where the Soviets feared that their FKR-2 cruise missiles would be spotted, and then photographing SAM positions at Banes in the north. There was no warning of increases in the air defence threat, although all the US Navy Operation *Blue Moon* RF-8As that day reported

Cuban troops investigate the wreckage of Maj Rudy Anderson's U-2F, 56-6675, after a tragic end to the extra mission for which he volunteered. He was awarded the Air Force Cross posthumously (*Getty Images*)

AAA fire. In fact, Anderson was exposed to eight SA-2 sites, but news of the most recent batteries had not been passed to OL-X from the latest SAC RB-47H ELINT flights. Anderson's U-2 also lacked the System 12 radar warning receiver (RWR) and System 14 ECM packages, as they were still being tested.

The 'hawks' in the USA saw this as the first shot in an inevitable war, and demanded attacks on the SAM sites. Castro claimed ignorance, but suggested that a SAM commander (in this case, 507th Antiaircraft Missile Regiment commander Lt Col Ivan Gerchanov) might have unilaterally responded to his demand for better air defence results. U-2 pilots expected that there would at least be air strikes on the offending SA-2 batteries.

After a mission by five U-2s the following day, which was terminated when threat signals were received, all such flights were suspended. It was later learned that Gerchanov had indeed been ordered to launch the fatal SA-2, and that identical weapons had been fired, unsuccessfully, at Capt Jerry McIlmoyle's U-2 on 25 October. Anderson's U-2F had flown into the SA-2 battery's range, and the Soviet 'Spoon Rest' and 'Fan Song' radars were working unusually well. A standard three-missile salvo was fired at a range of around six miles, and at least two exploded close to the U-2, killing Anderson with shrapnel. Khrushchev blamed Castro, mistakenly believing that he controlled the missiles. Gen Pliyev, in Cuba, blamed Lt Gen Stepan Grechko, in charge of the island's air defences, who claimed that he had tried to secure permission before ordering Lt Col Gerchanov to fire.

Kennedy and McNamara were convinced that they would have to attack the SAM sites, but Khrushchev's offer to trade missiles arrived before the order to strike the batteries could be given. Unwittingly, Anderson may have been the catalyst that caused both Khrushchev and Kennedy to accept a deal. Grechko, despite disobeying Khrushchev's orders, received a mild reprimand.

After a pause while only tactical reconnaissance aircraft were allowed over the island, U-2 missions were reinstated at the rate of two per day after Khrushchev's climb down and the 28 October agreement to remove the missiles. Resuming on 4 November 1962, missions persisted into 1963, as did the efforts of Cuban Air Force MiG-21 pilots to intercept them. U-2 pilots were ordered to break off their flight if a MiG came within 40 miles of them.

In the closing weeks of 1962, Cuba's Soviet armaments were slowly removed, but U-2s were frequently engaged by 'Fan Song' and 'Spoon Rest' radars, and their pilots did not know that the SAM crews had been told not to fire. The CIA also demanded more close-up detail to establish whether Soviet personnel had evacuated all the military sites, and a final RF-8A mission was allowed on 5 June 1963, albeit with indecisive results. However, the ongoing U-2 imagery provided overall evidence of the dismantling and shipping out of the Il-28 bombers and many of the missiles, although some remained for longer, as did the SA-2s.

The 4080th SRW achieved record mission rates and film handling times during the crisis. Indeed, its U-2s photographed more than 95 per cent of Cuba in 1962, for which the unit received the Presidential Unit Citation during a visit to Laughlin by Kennedy.

One U-2F mission on 20 November 1963 ended disastrously, with the loss of Capt Joe Hyde. He was returning from a *Brass Knob* Type B camera mission over Cuba in 56-6683, normally a reliable jet, when his autopilot failed at 69,000 ft. As he hand-flew the aircraft towards Barksdale AFB control was lost, presumably due to a stall, and the U-2 entered a flat spin, diving into the sea 40 miles south of Key West. SC-54D SAR aircraft were on the scene within ten minutes, and the film cassettes were recovered by divers from the wreckage, but no trace of Hyde was ever found.

In April 1964 Castro was still boasting that he would shoot down any U-2 that violated his airspace. Two or three weekly missions were flown without opposition, and the U-2 pilots later learned that Kennedy's successor, President Lyndon B Johnson, had warned Castro of dire consequences if U-2s were fired at.

Overflights of Cuba continued into 1966, when Capt Robert Hickman was lost in bizarre circumstances on a flight to verify removal of weapons from Cuba. His aircraft (56-6719) left Barksdale AFB at 0400 hrs on 28 July, provided some interception practice for 479th Tactical Fighter Wing (TFW) F-104Cs at NAS Key West but did not complete a planned turn to the east near Cuba and continued to head southeast. Attempts to contact Hickman yielded only silence. Two VMFA-531 F-4B Phantom IIs took off from Key West to try and intercept the U-2, but they were unable to reach it as it began to fly over Cuba.

The 'Dragon Lady' continued a stately southeasterly journey for more than 3000 miles on autopilot, crossing Panama, where an RB-57 tried to meet it and assess the situation. However, the aircraft could only climb to 10,000 ft below the U-2, which eventually ran out of fuel, entered a steep dive, lost a wing and crashed onto a 14,000-ft mountain south of La Paz, Bolivia. Hickman was believed to have had a stroke or haemorrhage, as he had been complaining of severe headaches for two days prior to his flight.

Another odd incident occurred near Barksdale on 1 July 1967 when Capt Sam Swart, flying U-2C 56-6708 from Laughlin, had to eject at 45,000 ft following an engine explosion. He was able to open his parachute at 10,000ft and land in open country. Swart set off along a road, but his other-worldly appearance in a pressure suit made one motorist accelerate away in alarm, rather than picking him up, while a young woman at a mobile home that he approached slammed the door in his face.

By the end of 1967, the 100th SRW U-2s at Barksdale were still required to provide photo coverage of almost all of Cuba every two months. In March 1969, under the codename *Glass Lamp*, Cuban overflights commenced from McCoy AFB with U-2Rs, but they were briefly suspended following the loss of EC-121M SIGINT aircraft 'Deep Sea 129' of US Navy squadron VQ-1 to North Korean MiG-21s over the Sea of Japan on 15 April 1969.

In mid-1970, the Cuban overflights were renamed *Old Head*, flown by U-2Rs from McCoy (OL-19, but renamed OL-RD) and reduced in frequency to one every 90 days. From August 1972 they were flown instead from Davis-Monthan AFB as *Olympic Fire* missions. The sorties continued until 1974, with pilots facing attempted interception by Cuban MiG-21s on a number of occasions. The appearance of a Soviet naval vessel in Cuban ports in 1972 caused an increase in surveillance flights, and the transfer of an additional U-2R to Davis-Monthan. From the autumn of 1974 the Cuban photo-reconnaissance task passed to the SR-71.

CHAPTER FOUR

GLOBAL REACH

A crew member indicates that pogos have been fitted to a U-2A-1, ready for the aircraft to taxi back to its dispersal area at either Plattsburgh or Ramey following an Operation *Crowflight* mission. The F-2 HASP extension to the Q-bay door is prominent here. The exact identity of this U-2 remains a mystery, for the '6671' serial on the fin is spurious. The real 56-6671 was an X-15. The entire tail section of the U-2 could be removed for engine access. The J57 was a very tight fit inside the fuselage, and difficult to install or remove (*USAF*)

Public revelation of the U-2 was suppressed by the CIA until February 1957, but as the aircraft moved out into the world, preserving the secrecy surrounding their operations had already become difficult. The 'Shady Lady's' unparalleled intelligence-gathering powers necessitated covert forward OLs all over the world. Many were temporary, and subject to fluctuating local political situations, while others remained as permanent launching points for worldwide coverage to respond to strategic needs. All required complex support facilities to enable U-2 sorties to be flown.

Crucial in all cases were the physiological support groups that prepared pilots for flight. For the 4080th SRW, its personal equipment group of 30 technicians worked with a medical group of 25 flight surgeons and assistants. Some would usually be on temporary duty (TDY) at one of the OLs at any time, providing pilots with the same support they would find at home. All pilots received a comprehensive physical examination before each flight. They ate a high protein meal (steak and eggs being favourite) and then 'suited up' – a complex process involving white long johns, the pressure suit and custom-fitted helmet and a parachute.

An hour on a recliner pre-breathing pure oxygen removed nitrogen from the pilot's bloodstream, thus preventing him from suffering 'the bends' at altitude. The 'driver' then entered the van taking him to his aircraft, with a 'navigator' carrying his portable oxygen supply that lasted for 30–45 minutes. Once installed in the cockpit, he was connected to the aircraft's oxygen system, radio and other facilities, ready to go through his checklists with the mobile pilot who oversaw his take-off. Briefing for U-2 flights invariably required two pilots. A second pilot went through the same physiological routines and mission preparation, and he would take over if the primary pilot did not meet the medical targets on the day.

The reserve pilot also prepared the cockpit and did the 'walk around' pre-flight inspection. Groundcrew strapped the pilot in, and in a recess to his right side stored his 'feast' that consisted of astronaut-style 'toothpaste tubes' with a nozzle that inserted through an airtight valve in the lower part of the helmet. A small, cylindrical food heater was available, and the menu comprised a range of delicacies which did not appeal to all tastes.

U-2R/TR-1 pilot Maj Steve Randle found the contents 'unappetising. Having never used the food heater before, I decided I ought to experience it just once, so I took along a new soup – clam chowder. I have to count it as a great success because the tube didn't explode as they sometimes did [in the food heater]. So I used it exactly once. I would never use it again'. Fellow pilot Maj Bob Uebelacker also bypassed the food heater. 'I'd stick to the apple sauces, peaches and pears. Beef and gravy just went to my stomach.' For other pilots, the tube food interrupted the boredom of long flights on autopilot, as did the reading material and music that many took aboard or, more recently, had beamed up to them via datalink.

At such high altitudes, as Col Mason Gaines pointed out, 'the sun was your enemy. You could literally feel the heat through the sleeves of the pressure suit if you rested your arms on the canopy rails, so remaining in the shade was important for staying cool. The pressure suit had air constantly circulating through it, and that was your primary climate control'. All U-2s had a 'sunshade' – originally white and later black – above the canopy, and a sliding panel inside the canopy that could be angled to blot out direct sunlight. 'The sliding panel was a help, although it was sometimes removed for a night flight', recalled Gaines. 'Our map boards and navigation log also became good sunshades, and could be positioned around the cockpit to cover up the sun.'

Sudden temperature changes at altitude could be a serious hazard because Mach number was linked to temperature, and the autopilot could suddenly pitch the aircraft up or down to follow the 'isotherm' line of correct temperature for the required Mach number, overstressing the airframe.

U-2 pilots had to adhere to a strict flight plan, keeping to within 500 ft of the prescribed altitude and with wings level to within three degrees of the horizon. The route had to be maintained to within three nautical miles of the planned flightpath. Over tropical areas, the U-2 was more likely to leave heavy contrails – the easiest way of detecting it from the ground even with the aircraft at 70,000 ft. A U-2 pilot could only see his contrail in his external mirror, which was not fitted to all aircraft.

SAMPLERS

Early SAC U-2 pilots were not allowed to overfly the same sensitive global areas as the CIA contingent. Instead, they were allocated unglamorous tasks from 1957 for the worldwide High-Altitude Sampling Programme

(HASP), collecting evidence of nuclear weapons tests in Operation *Crowflight*. More than 100 atmospheric nuclear tests by the USA, USSR and Great Britain were undertaken from 1945 through to 1963, when the Limited Test Ban Treaty moved them underground.

Six 'hard nose' U-2A-1s flew long missions twice weekly from Plattsburgh AFB, New York, and Ramey AFB, Puerto Rico, over Canada and the Atlantic at altitudes between 45,000–70,000 ft collecting dust samples. The tropical climate of Puerto Rico made correct engine trimming difficult, so there were numerous flameouts. U-2As had F-2 lower Q-bay hatches containing six 15-inch diameter sampling papers that were extended one at a time into a duct below the hatch to collect atmospheric dust particle. A 16 mm camera in the bay photographed a panel on which altitude, temperature, speed and other parameters were displayed.

Crowflight was followed by *Toy Soldier*, gathering samples from Soviet tests that would provide accurate details of the weapons involved. External P-2 'ball sampling' kits were supplied for attachment to new Q-bay doors. U-2s of the Eielson-based 4080th SRW flew daily sorties to collect samples that were internally stored within the aircraft in six pressurised spheres, as well as on filter papers. The CIA's Det C from Atsugi received the first sampling kits, and the 4080th followed later in 1957, with its U-2As at Eielson flying daily collection sorties to the northwest of Alaska during early 1958.

Returning U-2s were sometimes 'hot' with gamma radiation, requiring a thorough wash-down before they could be refuelled. Pilots were equipped with dosimeters to measure radiation they might have been exposed to in flight. 1Lt Mike Styer, who had flown through a radiation cloud over Siberia, had to remain in his cockpit for two hours while his U-2 was washed down.

Additional *Crowflight* sorties were made over the South Atlantic, some from Det 4 at Ezeiza airport near Buenos Aires, in Argentina, by three 'hard nose' U-2s fitted with P-2 units that spent almost 12 months there from September 1958 studying the long-term behaviour of fallout from nuclear tests conducted that year. They orbited from northern Brazil down to the Falkland Islands. In September 1960 *Crowflight* U-2As

'Smokey Joe', a cigar-wielding American Indian, adorns U-2D 56-6721, one of the purpose-built D-models for Air Research and Development Command's Special Project into detecting incoming ICBMs. The 1959 plan was for up to 15 U-2Ds to be airborne from Japan to Norway, ready to warn a ground station complex of missile threats from high altitude. Following service with Air Research and Development Command, 56-6721 flew from Edwards AFB until it was retired in 1978 and moved to the March AFB museum. The aircraft was later transferred to Palmdale, and it has been on display at the site's Blackbird Airpark for many years (*Terry Panopalis Collection*)

from Det 3 (Ramey) and Ezeiza (Det 4) were moved to Minot AFB, North Dakota, and Laughlin (Det 10) to survey the atmosphere in the northern hemisphere. Regular flights from Ramey continued periodically, however, and in December 1963 it hosted Det G U-2s for six flights in Operation *Seafoam*, the aircraft monitoring Cuban-inspired insurgent activity in Venezuela and British Guiana.

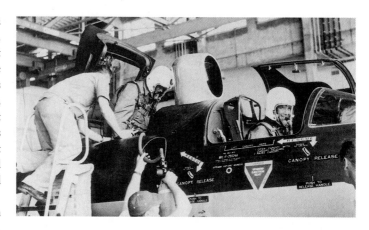

The pilot of 'Smokey Joe' U-2D (56-6721) seems far happier than the observer who is being 'incarcerated' in the very cramped extra Q-bay cockpit to operate the rotating 'Pickle Barrel' sensor immediately in front of his helmet. Its 'hot eye' lens and built-in spectrometer detected IR exhaust emissions from incoming ICBMs. The observer/operator had a CRT to monitor magnetic fields, but his vision of the outside world was limited to two small windows above his head (*Lockheed/Terry Panopalis Collection*)

When Soviet nuclear testing in Siberia resumed in September 1961, the frequency of *Toy Soldier* sorties from Eielson and Laughlin increased to two a day, and by October sampling kept half of SAC's U-2 fleet occupied. Tests included coverage of the USSR's colossal 50 megaton *Tsar Bomba*, the most powerful nuclear weapon ever detonated (on 30 October 1961). Shock waves from it circled the world three times.

Some air sampling sorties flown from Anderson AFB (OL-14), Guam, in 1962 were interrupted in November by Typhoon *Karen*, the most powerful tropical storm to ever hit the island. Winds of 115 mph destroyed 95 per cent of the island's homes and badly damaged three of the 4080th Det's aircraft.

Following a decade of no aerial sampling in the wake of the Limited Test Ban Treaty of 1963, such missions resumed again in 1973 when China began more atomic tests at Lop Nor in June of that year. The 100th SRW modified a U-2R with a filter and gas sampling system and devices to locate clouds of nuclear particles. *Olympic Race* missions were flown from Torrejon, Spain, in July 1973 with a U-2R equipped with the F-4/P-5 sampling system. Others flew from U-Tapao and Osan (OL-OA), in South Korea, in 1974 using two U-2Rs. Seventeen flights from Osan and eight direct missions from Beale AFB were made in 1976, with others from Eielson AFB.

In October 1980, a large Chinese nuclear detonation required seven flights from Osan, Beale and Eielson. After each mission, the U-2R and pilot had to be hosed down for up to 30 minutes to remove contamination. On one, the bleed air passing through the pressure suit of pilot Capt Rick Bishop was so contaminated that the suit had to be destroyed. His U-2R, 68-10331, needed several days of scrubbing and hosing before it could fly again.

BASES AT HOME

After forming at Turner AFB in April 1956, the 4080th SRW moved to Laughlin AFB in April 1957 and then to Davis-Monthan AFB in 1963. It became the 100th SRW in June 1966, including the 99th SRS which was based at U-Tapao Royal Thai Air Force Base (RTAFB), Thailand. The 100th SRW passed its nameplate to the KC-135 tanker wing at Beale when it moved there from Davis-Monthan in July 1976 to join the 9th SRW and operate alongside its SR-71s. By October of that year the move was

U-2A 56-6703 on a *Toy Soldier* mission, indicated by the artwork on the tail. Six *Toy Soldier* deployments, each requiring three U-2s, had been mounted by November 1960 for gas and particulate sampling. At the height of Soviet nuclear testing, more than half the U-2 fleet was involved in sampling missions (*USAF/Terry Panopalis Collection*)

complete, with the 99th SRS operating ten U-2Rs, two U-2CTs and the last five U-2Cs. Overseas operations continued from Osan as Det 2.

At home, Patrick AFB, Florida, was home to Det 5, with this site being the only permanent OL in the USA. It was a favourite location amongst U-2 air- and groundcrew for 70-day tours. Det 5 mounted *Olympic Fire* missions over Cuba until 1974, and others over Central and South America.

Det 3 continued to fly from Akrotiri, while OL-9 was established at Hickam, Hawaii, and in Central America, OL-18 was set up in 1962 at Howard AFB within the Fort Kobbe army complex in Panama, with Maj H E Melbratten as detachment commander. Minot AFB was used by Det 9 for *Crowflight* missions over the Arctic region in 1960. During one such sortie, U-2A 56-6716 would not re-start after a flame-out. When its battery subsequently exploded, Capt Roger Cooper decided to attempt a dead-stick landing on a frozen, snow-covered lake in Canada. He succeeded and was recovered by a rescue aircraft. The Royal Canadian Air Force cleared enough snow from the lake to allow the U-2A to take off and return to Minot. Shortly afterwards 56-6716 was converted into a U-2C.

AUSTRALIA

The first *Crowflight* high-altitude sampling sorties from Australia were flown from OL-11 at the Royal Australian Air Force (RAAF) base at East Sale, in southeastern Victoria, by 4080th crews after Argentina withdrew permission for basing at Ezeiza. Three 4080th SRW U-2As arrived at OL-11 for a two-months HASP deployment on 26 October 1960 following a 12-day flight from Laughlin via Hawaii. Four JB-57s were also despatched to East Sale for sampling at lower altitudes. Almost immediately after its formation at Davis-Monthan in March 1963, a 100th SRW group flew to Australia, where OL-11 was established for an enjoyable TDY at RAAF Laverton, near Melbourne. Another detachment, the last for *Crowflight* from OL-11, was there from June to September 1964, with personnel living in RAAF quarters and enjoying good facilities for its three U-2s. Sampling missions were flown towards the South Pole and back twice a week.

BRITAIN

After the first, short-lived CIA overseas U-2 deployment to RAF Lakenheath in April 1956, subsequent visits to Britain were conducted in a low-key manner, often using just a single aircraft. Det G briefly deployed U-2G 56-6681 to Upper Heyford, in Oxfordshire, in May 1967 for Operation *Scope Safe*. It was intended to overfly the Middle East, where the Six-Day War was imminent, before landing on board the carrier USS *Saratoga*

(CVA-60), as France had refused overflight rights. RAF pilots including Sqn Ldr Martin Bee were in line to make the flight, but the war began on 5 June and the British Labour government was then unwilling to have a US 'spyplane' in the country. The U-2G returned to the USA on the night of 7 June.

Scope Saint 1 in October 1968 involved U-2G 56-6681 making another one-week visit to Britain. A second *Scope Saint* training exercise in April 1969 took a Det G U-2R from Edwards AFB to St Mawgan, in Cornwall, to perform a sample operational mission, which had to be cancelled due to damage to the aircraft. *Scope Saint III* was flown by RAF pilot Sqn Ldr Dick Cloke to Kinloss, in Scotland, in October 1969 in a 12-hour trip. Several useful photographic sorties were then flown over the British Isles, and the principle of rapid deployment to British bases was proven.

In April 1975, British-owned Diego Garcia, in the Indian Ocean, provided a temporary base for a 99th SRS U-2R, detached from U-Tapao, to fly six *Senior Book* SIGINT missions over Somalia, where the Soviet Union had constructed a military base. Mildenhall, in Suffolk, was visited by *Senior Book*-configured U-2R 68-10336 in August 1976 for two NATO exercises, and another aircraft spent four months there in 1977 flying *Olympic Flame* SIGINT missions along the German border. In June 1978, U-2R 68-10339 visited Mildenhall for *Senior Ruby* ELINT trials, and upon returning to Lockheed's Palmdale plant, in California, it had *Senior Spear* SIGINT sensors added to its datalink capability. Other SIGINT/ELINT/COMINT (communications intelligence) missions took the Mildenhall Det aircraft out over the Arctic Circle to eavesdrop on Soviet emissions, data-linking to a ship-borne relay station.

U-2R 68-10339 was followed by 68-10338 with *Senior Book* equipment in September, returning in March 1979 for the establishment of Det 4 at Mildenhall. That became the second operational base for U-2 pilots after an initial posting to Osan.

CYPRUS

As previously noted, the RAF base at Akrotiri was used as a CIA OL in 1962 when the commander was Arthur Leatherwood and there were three assigned pilots, Tony Bevaqua, Robert Pine and Dave Ray. The secrecy of their operations meant that they occupied a separate area of the airfield and did not integrate with the RAF personnel. In 1970, CIA U-2Rs returned to monitor the Arab–Israeli conflict using the Type H camera, but Egypt eventually had these flights suspended. After the Yom Kippur War in October 1973, U-2R imagery of the battle zone between Israel and Egypt was collected in Operation *Olive Harvest* to show that both sides were keeping to the agreed ceasefire limits.

The single (by agreement with the Cypriot government) U-2R flying from Akrotiri was equipped with an Optical Bar Camera, and it was operated in as much secrecy as possible to avoid exacerbating the fragile political situation on the island. As a long-term side effect of the Frank Powers incident, the presence of a black U-2 could by then cause offence almost anywhere in the world. Akrotiri was known as OL Olive Harvest, or OL-OH, and unofficially as 'Fantasy Island'. A British Vauxhall car was used as 'chase' for the landing U-2, but it lacked the high speed of its American drag-racer counterparts.

Akrotiri was notorious for its crosswinds, which caused no trouble for aircraft with conventional three-point undercarriages, but U-2 pilots had to cope with it as there were no diversion bases. They learned to drag the down-wind wingtip on the runway to stop the wind from 'weathervaning' the aircraft off the tarmac.

In October 1973, a second U-2R had been pre-positioned at Upper Heyford for Operation *Forward Pass* flights over the Yom Kippur battlefield, recovering to Akrotiri or a Sixth Fleet carrier. Political vacillation delayed its first operational flight past the 23 October ceasefire, and the U-2R returned, unused, to the USA. However, its pilot, Jerry Shilt flew back on 12 May 1974 to complete the final *Olive Harvest* mission – the last in Project *Idealist*, which had lasted 14 years.

For 9th SRW U-2R pilots, Akrotiri was home to Det 3, and they were usually deployed there after a period at Mildenhall. The U-2R's Middle East commitment continued, with monitoring flights following the March 1979 peace treaty between Israel and Egypt running to eight or ten sorties per month by 1980.

FAR EAST

In the Far East, Weather Squadron (Provisional) 3 (WRSP-3, or Det C) had been established at Atsugi by the CIA in March 1957. It collected electronic and visual U-2 imagery categorised as 'National Level' from overflights of China, North Korea and the Soviet Union. Like other overseas U-2 detachments, it was supported by Det G at Edwards, which provided research and development innovations and tests to keep the aircraft viable. The missions continued the hazardous work of the 6007th Reconnaissance Group (Provisional) RB-50 and RB-45 crews, who had made their last pass over Vladivostok in December 1956. Strict security was maintained at the WRSP-3 facility so that even the Japanese government was not informed of the U-2 activity. However, the unit was understandably unaware of the inadvisability of appointing Pvt Lee Harvey Oswald to its US Marine Corps security detail.

Det C flew 30 nine-hour *Robin Hood* missions from Cubi Point, in the Philippines, for an unsuccessful CIA-supported rebel army opposing President Sukarno of Indonesia in 1958. Oddly, during the conflict two U-2 pilots, Carmine Vito and James Cherbonneaux, who had experience of World War 2 fighters, were detached to fly F-51 Mustangs with a CIA-sponsored air force supporting the rebel troops.

Det C appeared over the Taiwan Straits for the 1958 confrontations with China and also over Tibet in 1959 for Operation *Mill Town* in support of a planned CIA-sponsored Tibetan resistance to

Photographed in their hangar, four of the CIA's U-2As are secured from prying eyes while assigned to Det A at Atsugi during 1957. The closest aircraft (at right) represents what is most likely the world's very first 'low observable' treatment used on a U-2, the paint covering the bottom of the airframe being a ferrite-impregnated material that absorbed the radiated energy for hostile radar. Some of the U-2As feature NACA markings and others USAF weather squadron insignia. During training flights, these aircraft carried non-classified weather research instrumentation in case a pilot was forced to land at an unsecure location (*James C Goodall Collection*)

Chinese encroachment. Overflights of Vietnam and Laos were added in 1960. The latter yielded some surprises for Washington such as the unexpected detection of numerous tanks near Ban Ban, in Laos. Det G, flying from Takhli RTAFB, undertook five missions over the Sino-Indian border area in 1963, refuelling over India and photographing the build-up of communist forces on the Indian border.

Control of all U-2 activity, including handling of the resultant imagery (code-named *Chess*) and intelligence, was conducted under the overall definition *Talent*. That included the 67th Reconnaissance Technical Squadron (RTS) at Yokota, Japan, from July 1957, whose Overseas Processing and Interpretation Center (OPIC) had responsibility for the processing and dissemination of U-2-generated material from WRSP-3, managed by a *Talent* Control Officer. The unit's geographical area of responsibility covered the eastern Soviet Union, China and all of Southeast Asia, although data from the USSR was usually confined to flights around its coast.

Between March 1959 and March 1962, six *Talent* U-2 missions were managed by the 67th RTS, but after Powers' loss in May 1960 on a *Talent* flight, sorties were confined to a few flights over Manchuria, North Korea and China. Another OPIC was established with the 497th RTS at Schierstein, in West Germany, to manage U-2 imagery from the Middle East.

Producing useable imagery from traditional film was clearly based on accurate processing of the original negatives, from which high-resolution and three-dimensional prints could be made. Given that the value of photo intelligence to commanders was usually dependent on the speed with which it could be provided to them, the 67th RTS had to perfect rapid, accurate processing with speedy initial interpretation of the thousands of feet of data-laden celluloid produced by each sortie.

The 548th RTS at Showa, near Yokota, performed a similar function until January 1960, when its assets were transferred to the 67th RTS and it was eventually inactivated. Outside the Far East, the 497th RTS processed U-2 data for the Suez Crisis.

As noted earlier, the 67th RTS had the first Pacific OPIC. Two teams were formed from the 67th in 1957, with one 'Special Ops' unit supporting U-2, RB-45 and RB-57 operations, and the second, Det 2, deploying to Clark AB, in the Philippines, to support CIA U-2 flights from the US Navy station at Subic Bay during the civil unrest in that area. A six-man CIA team was sent to Clark to operate Det 2 (OPIC-X), accessing documentary reconnaissance material from the Showa laboratory. An OPIC manager was sent out from Washington ahead of any planned U-2 flights to manage the resultant film securely. Prodigious quantities of film were processed, usually at night, in quite primitive conditions and sent to the CIA in a C-47 for evaluation.

The general shortage of qualified lab technicians at the time meant long shifts for the few who were available. PIs examined the film, preferring prints to negatives, using Richards Light Tables which could handle the Hycon Model HR-73B Type B camera's 9 x 18-inch frames. When a mission-load of film was delivered, the laboratory had to work on it day and night until it was all processed, printed and examined. Eye-strain was normal, and operators had to wear face masks, paper hats and cotton gloves to minimise 'human pollution' of the delicate negatives.

At Yokota's top security Building 206, the U-2 lab behind the 'Green Door' had seven processing machine operators working with barely adequate, noisy A-9 equipment on film whose origins were unknown to them. Until Powers' crash in 1960, most 'Recce Tech' personnel knew hardly anything about the U-2. Even its maximum altitude was obscured for them by a mathematical adjustment formula. Security extended to the installation of a white noise-generating radio in the Quonset hut adjoining the labs to disguise breaktime conversations.

Initially, the imagery came from the U-2A's A-3 camera rig in the form of split-vertical exposures, but the introduction of the U-2C's complex Type B camera fit required very different processing, for which the 67th RTS was unprepared. Each of the cameras' two large metal magazines contained around a mile of film, producing paired images from cameras working in a different aiming cycle than the A-3. Titling of the negative frames was provided by an automatic Eastman Kodak machine. Locating the sites of each exposure on the ground was facilitated by the U-2's 70 mm tracker panoramic camera, which was switched on throughout the flight and recorded the entire flightpath.

Typically, the Pacific theatre was usually the destination for new U-2 pilots, who would be sent to Osan to undertake their first overseas deployment with the 9th SRW's Det 2. Using two U-2Rs and a Type H camera, they flew daily *Olympic Game* photo and SIGINT missions over the Demilitarized Zone using E-Systems' *Senior Spear* sensors in the wing pods.

Det 2 lost U-2R 68-10333 on 22 May 1984 when the tailpipe separated from the engine shortly after take-off from Osan, blowing off the rear section of the aircraft. Capt Dave Bonsi ejected and the aircraft was replaced by 80-1075 – one of the first U-2Rs from the new TR-1A/U-2R production line. TR-1A 80-1072 was lost at Beale on 18 July 1984 with rear fuselage failure, and this fate befell U-2R 80-1075 from Osan on 8 October. Both pilots survived ejection, although Capt Tom Dettmer of Det 2 almost drowned when he landed in a fast-flowing stream of icy water, weighed down by his parachute. After a period of grounding for the U-2R fleet, stronger attachments for the tailpipe were installed in all aircraft.

Chase cars varied according to the location of the base and the era. By the 1980s, Beale had five-litre Ford Mustangs, easily capable of 130mph, while Osan used a Chevrolet El Camino coupé utility that had had its engine tuned so that it produced more than 300 hp. This vehicle had replaced the previous Osan El Camino whose engine produced 400 hp. It required more than 300 lbs of sandbags in its cargo bed to stop the tyres from being worn too quickly. The coupé utility regularly pursued the two resident U-2Rs – *Senior Book* 68-10337 with a Type H camera fitted, and 'slick wing' 68-10331 without 24-ft long 'superpods'. The latter had detachable fore and aft sections to accommodate a variety of antennas and extra radomes in fairings under the pods.

MIDDLE EAST, PAKISTAN AND BEYOND

Det A at Wiesbaden was given new missions after Eisenhower suspended Soviet overflights in July 1956. U-2s now went instead to Egypt and the Middle East after President Gamal Abdel Nasser seized the Suez Canal.

Two U-2s provided imagery of the Canal Zone which was passed to the British government. Pilots, including Frank Powers, could watch Israeli and Egyptian tank battles through their Baird drift sights. Eisenhower, unaware that the British and French were planning to retake the canal by force, did not realise that the photographs would be used to plan an invasion of Egypt, although many of the U-2 images showed the build-up of British air assets in Cyprus and Malta and French fighter transfers to Israel. After the invasion, Eisenhower stopped further U-2 imagery from being passed on.

Daily U-2 flights, including one by Powers over Egypt after the invasion on 5 November 1956, revealed the damage caused by British and French air attacks. Other flights covered countries around the Mediterranean including Syria, Cyprus, Israel and Jordan. U-2s recovered to Incirlik, and their imagery was processed there by the 497th RTS. Incirlik had by then replaced Wiesbaden as the European U-2 base (Det A's three U-2s were subsequently transferred to Laughlin in November 1956, giving the 4080th a peak strength of 18 aircraft), with Det B having commenced operations from there on 11 September 1956. Its eight pilots had only completed their U-2 course at 'The Ranch' the previous month.

Det B U-2As were airlifted out in C-124s and re-assembled at Incirlik, where the unit was supported by Det 1010. Its first flight on 11 September was a six-hour affair over the Suez Canal Zone, undertaken by Maj Harry N Cordes. He surveyed British and French naval forces and bases in the area from 70,000 ft. On his return, the engine flamed out (a common problem), and Cordes had to descend to 35,000 ft to restart it – the standard altitude for this procedure using battery power if the engine was windmilling at 35 per cent speed.

Det B flew daily sorties over the battlefields during the Suez Crisis, followed by tactical reconnaissance flights over Lebanon in 1958, completing 168 missions by May 1960. The imagery captured went through three stages of interpretation: the Initial Photographic Interpretation Report evaluated the accuracy of coverage of the intended target areas; a Supplemental Photographic Interpretation Report (SUPIR) went into more detail; and a third phase yielded expert reviews of specific installations such as a nuclear test centre or missile launch site.

After Suez, Det B had a fairly quiet period, performing a few Soviet overflights and peripheral intelligence sorties. In May 1957 a mobile unit was moved to Lahore, with the intention of resuming more intensive overflights of the USSR. U-2s were ferried there, one of them by Frank Powers, who made a perfect dead-stick landing at Lahore after a flame-out.

Some requests for U-2 surveillance only required a single mission. A December 1980 flight from Mildenhall photographed a devastating earthquake in southern Italy. Another in January 1980 provided the Saudi government with imagery of the conflict between North Yemen and the Soviet-sponsored South Yemeni fighters. In February 1976, two flights were made to survey the results of an earthquake in Guatemala, while El Salvador came under the 'Dragon Lady's' watchful eyes in 1980 to see how Marxist insurgents were receiving weapons.

The introduction of in-flight refuelling in 1960 with the advent of the U-2C vastly increased its ability to penetrate large areas of hostile terrain, although the refuelling process was usually challenging for both tanker crews and 'Dragon Lady' pilots (*USAF*)

CHAPTER FIVE

'BLACK CATS'

Maj 'Mike' Hua Hsi-chun's U-2A 56-6721 after his deadstick landing and ground loop at Cortez airport on the night of 3 August 1959. The aircraft was repaired and converted into a U-2D two-seater for the 'Smokey Joe' project (see photograph on page 53). Eventually retired in 1978, 56-6721 has resided at the Blackbird Airpark at Palmdale for many years (*USAF*)

Of all the U-2 pilots who braved Soviet SA-2 missiles, the 27 Republic of China Air Force (RoCAF) photo-reconnaissance pilots, nicknamed the 'Black Cats', were subjected to the most frequent attacks, and losses. Indeed, their first loss was also the initial combat success for the SA-2, although that was not realised at the time. Moscow had supplied five SA-2 battalions with 62 missiles and expert advisors to China from 1958 before diplomatic relations between the two countries chilled.

On 7 October 1959, Capt Wang Ying Chin Wong's RB-57D (53-3978) was shot down near Peking (Beijing) by a salvo of three SA-2s. Wong was presumed killed, but there was no knowledge of the arrival of the SA-2s and no communication from the RB-57D. It was therefore assumed that he had been intercepted by fighters, even at his altitude of 63,000 ft, or to have sustained a mechanical failure.

Nationalist Chinese pilots had been flying RB-57 high-altitude reconnaissance missions over mainland China since 1956, sharing their photographic and electronic intelligence with the CIA. The ongoing threat of invasion of Formosa (Taiwan) by mainland China came to a head in 1958 with recurring aerial battles between RoCAF F-86s and communist Chinese MiG-17s. By year end, US forces on Formosa included the 4028th SRS equipped with RB-57Ds from Yokota that could reach 66,000 ft, and three were transferred to RoCAF service in Project *Diamond Lil*. Moscow had provided the SA-2 systems secretly to counter these high-flyers.

The RB-57Ds achieved some dramatic revelations with their K-38 cameras, notably the deployment of an SA-2 battery to Wuchang, China, in September 1958, although its significance was not appreciated at the time. More were discovered by Corona satellite surveillance. Wing fatigue soon grounded the final RB-57D, making the U-2 a clear choice for continued surveillance work.

US forces were becoming increasingly involved in Southeast Asia, so monitoring China and the Taiwan Straits stretched their reconnaissance assets. CIA U-2s from Det C at Atsugi surveyed the coast of China in September–October 1958 to assess the likelihood of a Chinese invasion of Taiwan. The first flight, by Lyle Rudd, photographed 13 airfields, but none of the missions detected a significant build-up of forces. Other missions followed in May 1959, and in one, Rudd flew from Cubi Point, surveyed the Koko Nor area bordering Tibet and the nuclear research facilities at Lop Nor and Shuang-Cheng-Tzu, before finally landing at Tejgaon, in East Pakistan (now Bangladesh). He then returned to Cubi Point.

It made sense to train RoCAF pilots on the U-2A to provide additional intelligence for the CIA, which could also claim deniability in the event of a loss. One CIA pilot would be assigned to the squadron to maintain flight standards, and the CIA would provide maintenance and control of all intelligence collected by the U-2s.

Training of six former RoCAF fighter pilots at Laughlin AFB began in April 1959 without the benefit of a two-seat U-2 or even flight manuals in Mandarin. Pilots were required to have 2000 hrs of flying time, preferably in fighters, a reasonable command of English and a reputation for courage – which they would certainly need. They chose English nicknames, and local people were told that they were Hawaiian. Three U-2s were written off, mainly due to misunderstandings about flight procedures.

Maj 'Mike' Hua Hsi-chun experienced one of the first mishaps, on 3 August 1959. While flying U-2A 56-6721 on his first night navigation training mission, he had a flameout at 70,000 ft over Colorado. Several attempts at re-starting failed and he descended through cloud to make an emergency landing. In fact, the fuel system had malfunctioned and his remaining fuel had been dumped. As he broke through the cloud, he found himself flying down a narrow valley with high mountains on either side, heading towards Cortez airport, the only airfield for 100 miles around. He was also lined up on the runway beacon and lights which were, unusually, left on at night.

Hua lowered his landing gear and circled the lights, preparing to land. He then noticed that he was approaching Cortez's main street, not the runway. Raising the landing gear, he turned towards the runway and attempted to lower it again, but with power off there was insufficient time and hydraulic pressure to re-extend it. He belly landed and ground-looped off the runway. Hua exited the U-2A and walked towards the small airfield office, still wearing his pressure suit and helmet. The airport manager immediately assumed that he was an alien. Hua, briefly unable to master spoken English, was eventually able to call for security for his U-2A.

Five pilots were back in Taiwan by September 1959, but disputes between the CIA and USAF over control of overflights of China delayed the start of operations. Richard Bissell, in charge of the CIA's U-2s, wanted Det C to manage the flights, support and training in Taiwan but SAC objected.

The CIA's specific purpose in supporting this venture was partly to acquire information on the Lop Nor nuclear development site in Sinkiang province, active since 1955, without risking CIA pilots. The Chiuchuan missile range in Kansu province and Shuang-Cheng-Tzu launch site were also of great interest. Six overflights of the Koko Nor research centre in northern China had already been made by US Det C pilots Tom Crull, Lyle Rudd and Bill McMurry from Takhli (at that stage a primitive CIA secret base) and Cubi Point between 12 May 1959 and 5 April 1960.

Rudd was the first U-2 pilot to overfly mainland China, reaching Peking and remaining in Chinese airspace for more than nine hours on 19 June, with Chinese fighters often in attendance below him. A repeat flight on 20 August showed that China had amassed large air forces on bases facing Taiwan, as did the final flight on 22 October, before protests from Peking and the CIA's failure to keep Eisenhower in the picture concerning the flights terminated further CIA-flown China missions.

Security concerns had been raised when Crull, who had been overflying 'denied territory' since May 1959 and was chased by MiGs on one occasion, ran short of fuel in U-2C 56-6693 (later to be lost with Powers aboard) on 24 September 1959. The aircraft's improved high-altitude endurance and higher power, even at the idle throttle setting, slowed its planned descent from a record 76,400 ft. He had to belly-land the unmarked, black-painted jet on a Japanese glider airfield, where it immediately became an attraction for camera-carrying civilians. Nervousness in Washington about overflights in general was duly increased.

CIA arrangements to establish Det H in Taiwan progressed ahead of White House approval on 15 November 1960. The 'sale' of two CIA U-2Cs (Articles 358/56-6691 and 378/56-6711, which were allegedly 'salvage' sold to Lockheed by the CIA) to the RoCAF was arranged on 7 October 1959, and later denied by President Kennedy after the first U-2 loss over China. The arrangement, code-named Project *Tackle* in December 1960 and backed by pilot training for Det H of the RoCAF's 35th Squadron, was overseen by Gen Fu-en I, RoCAF head of intelligence, managed by Lt Col Denny Posten (whose cover name was 'Danny Perling') and commanded by F-86 pilot Col Lu Yang, known as 'Gimo'.

Research and development backing came from Det G at Edwards AFB, and the unit adopted a 'Black Cats' logo and applied the 12-pointed star national insignia to its first two U-2Cs, which arrived in December 1960 aboard USAF C-133 Cargomaster transports. A further 17 U-2s would be delivered for RoCAF use. The 35th Squadron, commanded by Col Lu 'Michael' Xiliang, was formed in 1961 and tasked with 'high-altitude weather research'. The unit operated from a bomb-proof bunker called the 'Roman Temple' at Taoyuan, on the northern tip of Taiwan, and all CIA and US personnel assigned to the 35th were given assumed names and listed as Lockheed technical representatives.

Difficulty in mastering the 'Dragon Lady' caused the first fatality on 19 March 1961 when Maj Yao-hua Chih lost control of U-2C 56-6684 during night landing practice at Taoyuan. Nevertheless, the first mission in the programme codenamed *Church Door*, was flown by Maj Chen-

Huai Sheng over the secret Shuang-Cheng-Tzu and Koko Nor sites on 13 January 1962 for an 8 hrs 40 min 3320-mile sortie. Oblique Type B camera imagery of the missile test areas and an SA-2 site was recorded and sent to Yokota's 67th RTS. Chen avoided fighter interception, although he was tracked by radar.

The U-2Cs were equipped with STL/Ramo Wooldridge-manufactured SIGINT Systems 3 and 6 receivers, fitted to CIA U-2s to monitor VHF transmissions. System 6 required a 'scimitar'-shaped antenna in a slender rectangular radome beneath the rear fuselage. Like all similar electronic additions, it added weight and slightly reduced the aircraft's maximum altitude.

At first all film was processed in American labs, but after a CIA C-47 sustained engine failure en route to Washington and 43 boxes of U-2 film were jettisoned over mountains in Pennsylvania (all were recovered, eventually), permission was given to use the labs at Taoyuan under supervision from Eastman Kodak and Hycon.

The CIA had calculated that an SA-2 could probably reach the 'Dragon Lady's' operational altitude, and that a pilot's only defence on the early missions over China was to try and manoeuvre to evade an attack. However, the U-2's fragile structure and tight stall margin made this almost impossible. By June 1963 the Chinese had reverse-engineered the SA-2 as the HQ-1 Red Flag, although the accompanying 'Fan Song' radar system took until 1970 to copy successfully. Two of the three SAM battalions located around Peking were photographed by Maj Hua Hsi-chun as he overflew that city en route from a 'nuclear hunt' mission beyond Manchuria on 11 August 1962. The CIA knew little of the SAM deployment to China, relying on the occasional 'Black Cats' flights and limited coverage from satellites to detect their presence. Although Hua was tracked on radar, the missile crews were not ready to fire at him. China's limited SAM force had a vast area to cover, and they tried to move the transportable SA-2 batteries to areas where U-2 flights were anticipated.

The 9 September 1962 mission by recently promoted Lt Col Chen-Huai Sheng in U-2 56-6711 was tracked on radar as it overflew Nanjing and then returned on a reciprocal course. The standard salvo of three SA-2s was fired at this now very vulnerable U-2C, and the first 'Black Cats' aircraft was downed. Chen-Huai died from his injuries and Peking enjoyed a propaganda coup which forced the US government to admit that it had sold two U-2s to the RoCAF, without admitting any other involvement. Both US pilots working with the 'Black Cats' were pulled out by the CIA and flights by the three surviving Chinese pilots were suspended.

Early in 1963 all RoCAF U-2s had been fitted with ATI System 12B/C SAM-warning systems that identified the SA-2's RSNA-75 'Fan Song' fire control radar and broadly indicated the direction of the threat. 'Black Cats' flights had resumed in December 1962 following the installation of System 12, despite its warning function being of dubious value until later versions indicated the direction of a radar threat with more accuracy.

However, most plucky 'Black Cats' pilots survived the SA-2 threat, as well as failed interceptions by steadily improving Soviet interceptors like the supersonic MiG-19 'Farmer', which had entered service in June 1955 and attempted to intercept U-2s over East Germany from the autumn of 1957 – China produced a semi-authorised copy, the Shenyang J-6, from 1961.

A Soviet variant, the MiG-19SU, had a liquid fuel booster pack specifically to intercept the U-2, but the design was abandoned when the aircraft was found to be uncontrollable at high altitudes. On one occasion a pilot overflying China for *Church Door* in 1961 managed to bank steeply under threat, and his cameras recorded the afterburners of a zoom-climbing J-6 falling away beneath him, having missed its target. He continued with his mission.

Further carefully planned *Church Door* missions followed from 23 February 1962 after another U-2C was delivered, followed by a third in June. Lt Col 'Gimo' Shih-Chu Yang photographed the Lanzhou Uranium-235 plant, Shantou, mining at Koko Nor and an unexpected pair of Tu-16 heavy bombers at Wa Kung airfield. Again, radar followed 'Gimo's' long journey, but MiG-15 and MiG-17 fighters failed to reach the U-2C's altitude. By March the first high-altitude, Soviet-supplied MiG-21s were detected on six bases bordering North Vietnam beneath 'Black Cats' flights. The missile-armed fighters could climb to 60,000 ft, representing a more serious threat to U-2s than earlier MiGs. However, to attempt an interception meant accelerating to almost Mach 2 at around 45,000 ft before initiating a semi-ballistic zoom climb to release a missile.

These rare but very hazardous journeys over China's most heavily defended territory at the U-2C's extreme range inevitably brought losses. As previously noted, on 8 September 1962 following 14 unharmed missions, the first U-2 was hit over Nanjing by an SA-2 and Lt Col Chen-Huai Sheng was lost. The SA-2's effective range of up to 26 miles meant that U-2s cruising over China's vast territory had to pass close to a missile site for the SA-2 to be successful.

After a pause ordered by President Kennedy, the need for more information demanded the resumption of Chinese overflights. Training restarted in October, using the sole surviving U-2C, 56-6688, modified to prevent flame-outs and reduce risk of stalling. Missions resumed, only for the last remaining U-2C to be caught between three SAM batteries over Jiangxi Province on 1 November 1963. The aircraft was hit by a salvo from the 2nd SAM Battalion and Capt 'Robin' Yeh Chang-Di was thrown out of the disintegrating 'Dragon Lady'. He duly parachuted into 19 years of captivity, the majority of it spent in solitary confinement. 56-6688's RWR equipment was captured and carefully analysed.

Like Maj 'Jack' Chang Li-Yi, who was shot down over Inner Mongolia by the 1st SAM Battalion on 10 January 1965, Capt Yeh was released in November 1982, having been presumed to be dead. Both men were

After the loss of the Frank Powers U-2, the CIA decided that revelation of the aircraft in the USA was inevitable to reassure the public of its 'research' purpose. Test and development U-2A 56-6711, complete with a fake NASA tail band and serial ('55741'), was duly displayed to the Press at Edwards AFB. Eventually transferred to the 'Black Cats' squadron as a U-2C in early 1962, the aircraft was brought down by SA-2s over China on 9 September that same year with pilot Lt Col Chen-Huai Sheng at the controls (*AFFTC/Terry Panopalis Collection*)

considered to have dishonoured Taiwan by being captured and were refused re-entry into the country. The USA offered them sanctuary until their eventual repatriation in 1990.

A MiG-21 attempted to intercept Capt 'Charlie' Wu Tsai-Shi's U-2 on 14 March 1965 in a zoom climb close to his altitude, releasing two K-13 (AA-2 'Atoll') IR missiles that failed to lock onto the U-2. Anything more than a shallow turn to avoid a MiG-21, which would have been virtually unable to manoeuvre at that altitude, reduced the U-2's ceiling. A simple precaution against IR missiles was to lengthen the 'sugar scoop' extension beneath the U-2's tailpipe, hiding its heat signature from K-13s climbing towards the jet. If the U-2 could stay above 'contrail altitude', it would also be virtually invisible to a MiG-21 pilot.

When MiG-21s attempted to intercept 4080th SRW U-2Cs over North Vietnam, USAF fighters were tasked with providing escort for them at lower altitude. Such protection was unnecessary as the communist interceptors were invariably too far below the U-2 to intervene.

MiG-21F-13s were theoretically capable of attaining 80,000 ft, but their small fuel capacity meant that accurate pre-positioning at around 25,000 ft near to the U-2's expected flightpath was essential. If the ground controller and pilot could calculate a zoom interception correctly, the MiG pilot would have had only a few seconds to find the target and lock his missiles onto it. His jet would then tumble into denser air. Several Chinese MiG-21 pilots managed to pass within a short distance of 'Black Cats' U-2s, but they had insufficient time to set up their weapons. In USAF trials using F-104As from the 319th Fighter Interceptor Squadron, several interceptions were made at altitudes of up to 64,000 ft.

As a further protective measure, operational U-2s received the ultra-matt 'black velvet' paint scheme devised by the Pittsburgh Paint and Glass Company to absorb light better than standard black paint, and also reduce the aircraft's radar signature by means of tiny metallic 'balls' in the paint. At high altitude, fighter pilots had difficulty seeing the U-2 against the dark background of the upper atmosphere.

RoCAF 'Black Cats' missions for the rest of 1965 avoided the heavily defended atomic research plants and test areas of northwest China, leaving them to the KH-4 Corona satellites. However, there were many other areas for RoCAF U-2s to survey as the Vietnam War gathered pace, including the provinces bordering North Vietnam and Hainan Island from which communist Chinese fighters occasionally intercepted US aircraft entering North Vietnam or after they had made navigational errors.

A few *Tackle* missions also crossed, or surveyed, North Korea, checking on its increasing military resources. All missions were coordinated by the Joint Reconnaissance Center in the USA. Usually, the RoCAF U-2s flew around the borders of North Korea, avoiding known SA-2 batteries surrounding Pyongyang and the MiG-21s at Pyong Ni airfield. Two missions in October 1963 by Maj Tao 'Tiger' Wang and Lt Col 'Terry' Lee Nan-ping repeatedly overflew North Korean targets in a U-2 protected by a Granger System 9 deceptive jammer in its tail and a light-weight ATI System 12 SAM launch warning receiver.

Although comparatively little intelligence was typically gathered during these missions, Lt Col 'Terry' Liu Jet-Chang's 31 July 1965 sortie from

Long lines of Peking citizens view the sad remains of four of the five 'Black Cats' U-2s downed by SAMs. The ejection seats initially fitted to the aircraft had a poor reputation, and several US and RoCAF pilots were lost in failed bail-out attempts. U-2s tended to crash in a flat spin due to their light structure, hence the intact nature of these aircraft (*CIA/Terry Panopalis Collection*)

Taoyuan identified ten new locations, including the Nyongbyon nuclear research centre 60 miles north of Pyongyang where a nuclear energy plant was taking shape, with Soviet assistance. Some missions launched from or terminated at Kunsan.

Another stand-down was ordered after Capt Yeh's loss on 1 November 1963, but U-2 flights had to resume in 1964. On 7 July, Lt Col Lee Nan-ping (by then the only remaining RoCAF pilot capable of flying operational sorties in the aircraft, pending the arrival of two new trainees, and three more in 1965) flew from Cubi Point as part of a simultaneous three-aircraft intrusion from different directions. One of the other aircraft involved was a RoCAF RF-101A Voodoo, flying at low-altitude.

At the controls of U-2G 56-6695, recently returned from aircraft carrier trials, Lee photographed North Vietnamese supply lines from China and three targets in southern China. His aircraft had the Birdwatcher telemetry system installed, automatically sending basic flight data from the U-2 back to the command post in short, coded bursts so that Taiwan could track a sortie. It also had the new Itek System 112B twin stereo camera that required a 'bulged' Q-bay hatch.

Lee headed straight for the 2nd SAM Battalion site, where commander Yue Zhenhua's troops tracked the U-2 with an AAA range-finding radar. The Red Flag's 'Fan Song' radar was turned on at the last moment – too late for Lee's System 12 to give him adequate warning – and three SAMs were fired. One destroyed the U-2G and Lee was unable to bail out. Delaying the 'Fan Song' lock-on removed any possibility of evasive action by a U-2 pilot who would, in any case, be aware that strenuous manoeuvres would stall his aircraft or induce structural failure.

After another hiatus, flights by the small 'Black Cats' unit resumed on 31 October with improved System 13 ECM fitted to the U-2s. Three missions occurred in October and November 1964, following China's first nuclear test on 16 October. An experimental mission by Maj 'Jack' Chang Li-Yi in an aircraft with a Texas Instruments FFD-2 IR camera loaded into the Q-bay took place on 26 November to secure IR imagery of heat from uranium processing at the Lanzhou nuclear facility. By then the complex was protected by the expanded and very mobile 2nd SAM Battalion. Three Red Flags were fired at the U-2 at a distance of 25 miles, and Chang made a shallow descending turn as his launch warning receiver activated. All the SAMs self-destructed, jammed by the heavy but effective new Sanders System 13 ECM pods fitted in his U-2's slipper tanks, replacing much-needed fuel. It was a fruitless mission, but the self-protection had saved the U-2.

A follow-up mission by Maj 'Pete' Wang Chen-Wen on 8 January 1965 showed that the Lanzhou plant was the likely source of China's enriched uranium.

Chang flew again on 10 January, heading for the Baotau nuclear and industrial complex, in Inner Mongolia, with the IR camera. Three SAMs were fired at him at 68,000 ft from an undetected site. His Birdwatcher malfunctioned, and Chinese electronics technicians had installed a powerful transmitter at the Red Flag site using a different frequency to mask the 'Fan Song's' emissions from detection by Sanders System 13. Chang, therefore, had no warning of the two missiles that destroyed his U-2C (56-6691), and he was lucky to survive ejection, exposure to bitter temperatures and shrapnel injuries. He then spent 17 years in a Chinese prison. Chang's System 13 deceptive jammer in the aircraft's tail-end was sufficiently intact for Chinese technicians to analyse it and devise counter-countermeasures. By mid-1967, nine RoCAF pilots had been lost. Their families received financial compensation from the CIA.

Improvements for the U-2's ECM protection had been gradually developed in 1964, but the size of existing units had to be reduced to allow them to be installed in the weight-critical aircraft. 56-6718, originally a HASP U-2A, converted into a U-2G, was the first to feature the full-length dorsal fairing above the fuselage for System 9B jammers and System 12B RWR in 1965. The system's cockpit scope showed the direction of a 'Fan Song' threat and an aural alert warned of radar detection, whilst a red light (the 'OS' or 'Oh Shit' light) indicated that the 'Fan Song' had switched from 'standby' to 'launch' mode. Sanders redesigned their System 13A deceptive countermeasures set so that it would fit in the U-2's rear fuselage.

Lighter versions of the Hycon Type B camera were also developed, as were more versatile QRC-192 ELINT and System 17 SIGINT installations. Pilots also received better navigation computers, a Doppler radar and improved radios, with the updated aircraft arriving in Taiwan from April 1965.

'Black Cats' pilots had frequently faced mechanical problems as well as Chinese defences. Engine flame-outs due to contaminated fuel and inverter or fuel pump failures were common. If these occurred at operational altitude, the pilot had to descend to around 35,000 ft to attempt a re-light, putting himself in range of fighters and heavy AAA. MiGs usually followed every U-2 flight, flying well beneath them and hoping that a problem would bring the aircraft down to interception altitudes. Faulty manufacture of the bearings used in the electrical generators and wiring failures due to prolonged exposure to low temperatures caused occasional electrical power loss. Such a failure cut off the cameras, autopilot and SIGINT systems so that a pilot had to try and recover to a base relying on a standby battery. The autopilot itself was sometimes unreliable, occasionally signalling control movements that overstressed the airframe. The loss of Maj 'Pete' Wang Chen-Wen and U-2C 56-6685 on 22 October 1965 was attributed to structural failure after excessive autopilot control inputs.

The airframe's fragility was also demonstrated in the loss of the often-converted first production CIA U-2A/F 56-6675 during inflight refuelling training at Edwards AFB on 25 February 1966. A wing separated as pilot 'Deke' Hall climbed away from the tanker, applying excess positive 'g' and aileron input that overstressed the wings. U-2Cs 56-6708 and 56-6954

This wrecked U-2C, framed by two HQ-1 Red Flags, is claimed to be the aircraft of Maj 'Jack' Chang Li-Yi, who was shot down in Article 358 (56-6691) on 10 January 1965 by 1st Battalion SAMs near the Baotau nuclear and industrial complex. Chang was imprisoned for 17 years, and following his release he was refused re-entry into Taiwan by President Chiang Ching-kuo (*CIA/Terry Panopalis Collection*)

were also lost to structural failure of a wing in turbulent air. U-2F 56-6689, lost along with Maj 'Sonny' Liang Teh-pei, probably succumbed to structural failure after a sharp turn during a training flight over the Taiwan Strait.

Faulty engine instruments caused the loss of Capt 'Charlie' Wu Tsai-Shi and U-2F 56-6705 on 17 February 1966 at Taichung when he attempted a dead-stick landing after a false overheating indication but overshot and crashed. Although complete engine failure was quite rare, Capt 'Mickey' Yu Ching-Chang – one of the mid-1965 'Black Cats' additions – was lost on 21 June 1966 when U-2C 56-6717 shed a compressor disc on an overwater flight. He tried to glide back to Taiwan, reversed towards Okinawa and finally crash-landed on a small, rocky island. Yu's ejection at 300 ft was too late to save him.

For both 'Black Cats' and SAC pilots, the normal stresses of flying a U-2 were exacerbated by the lack of powered controls, tactical air navigation (TACAN) and instrument landing system (ILS) equipment – all omitted in the basic quest to keep the weight down.

The 67th RTS's OPIC-1 at Yokota was tasked with handling the 'Black Cats'' Type B camera footage that charted large areas of China not covered by CIA *Talent* or other top secret flights. Some of the film from these *Church Door* missions (flown within Project *Tackle*), begun in early 1962, was delivered by air on two large spools, processed and transferred as 250- or 500-ft batches in cans to be duplicated and shipped from Tachikawa AB, Japan. Most went for further analysis at SAC HQ at Offutt AFB or to CIA personnel in Washington, D.C.

Church Door flights, which would be made for another nine years, began on 13 January 1962, and that first sortie produced spectacular imagery of China's airfields, military emplacements and naval docks. The Lop Nor nuclear test area was included in the early *Church Door* target list. For the processors, the photographs from these missions was a pleasing relief from the endless *Talent* film of Laotian jungle that they were used to. Although the early KH-4 Corona satellite reconnaissance imagery became available from October 1962, its resolution was inferior to photography by the Type B camera, although its coverage was wider. Corona could identify target areas that warranted closer observation with high-resolution U-2 cameras, although it was often unable to identify missile batteries that could make those follow-up missions dangerous.

The frequency of U-2 sorties was stepped up, as they were providing, for the first time, a comprehensive portrait for the CIA of China's resources, including warning of the first Chinese nuclear bomb detonation – a *Church Door* mission to Lanzhou nuclear research centre had acquired useful pre-warning data.

Film from most U-2 *Talent* flights often had to be 'sanitised' in the lab, removing details of times, camera focal length and 'taking altitude' from duplicated imagery, particularly if it was to be sent to South Korean bases, where theft and spying were common around US facilities. The Type B camera photography from U-2Cs was the first imagery captured over North Korea since 1953, so it was particularly valuable. Occasionally, the lab team was told to blur the prints slightly so that any unauthorised viewers would not have an exact idea of the resolution capability of the U-2's high-altitude cameras.

By 1960 the 67th RTS was managing the Pacific Air Force's (PACAF's) film library, which contained the products of more than 200,000 Far East reconnaissance sorties that had yielded millions of images, each one a classified document. The huge amounts of wasted 9.5-inch film and leader had to be burned in furnaces or in the open in piles up to 12 ft high. 'Black Cats' and *Church Door* pilots were famous for exposing all the film they carried, requiring long extra lab shifts that could take up to four days to complete. Under pressure to get results back to those requiring them, original negative strips would sometimes get dragged across a gritty floor and scratched.

CIA money paid for upgrades to the Det H facilities at Taoyuan from 1967, including improved processing facilities, although some film was still processed at US bases.

When 'Black Cats' missions resumed in the early spring of 1966 after a four-month pause, Maj 'Spike' Chuang Jen-Liang's U-2C had at least two Red Flags fired at it over Kunming on 14 May. Observing the approaching missiles through his drift sight, Chuang engaged his System 13 jamming and made the recommended 30-degree evasive turn. The SAMs passed harmlessly behind him. With China's own Red Flag SA-2 copies now in production, the number of missile batteries increased to 21 by mid-1967. Although Chuang's U-2 had survived, there was another 12-week pause in missions pending delivery of the upgraded, automatic Sanders System 13C. U-2Cs were also fitted with a Granger Associates ECM box that jammed Soviet X-band fighter radars in the aircraft's rear quarter.

'Black Cats' missions were used to assess China's support for the Hanoi regime in 1965. Five missions were flown from Taoyuan to study Chinese logistics on the supply routes to North Vietnam, some flights starting or ending at Takhli.

In the summer of 1967 the CIA was still urgently seeking information on the Lop Nor nuclear test site. In Project *Tabasco*, two U-2 flights were made, dropping sensor pods near the area. The Sandia-designed, ten-feet-long pods were carried on the U-2's drop tank attachment points. They were supposed to land by parachute, partially bury themselves in soft ground and transmit SIGINT data from Lop Nor to a CIA station in Taiwan.

Maj 'Spike' Chuang Jen-Liang, in U-2C 56-6716, made the first attempt on 7 May in a 1800-mile flight from Takhli, but the pods never activated and his tracking camera failed, so that there was no evidence of the drop. On 31 August, an equally unsuccessful repeat mission was flown by Lt Col 'Billy' Chang Hseih in the same U-2C. It carried an extending antenna to check whether the pods were working. Chang's System 13 protected him from six SAMs, one exploding around 3000 ft away. His antenna picked up signals, but they were not from the pods.

Although Chang's ECM had worked well, a fifth U-2C (56-6706) was shot down near Shanghai on 9 September 1967 with the loss of Capt 'Tom' Huang Yun-pei, flying his first mission. Chinese countermeasures eventually overcame his System 13 after it had jammed SAM sites around Shanghai for more than 30 minutes. One of the three Red Flags launched by the 14th SAM Battalion destroyed the 'Dragon Lady'. There was another pause in operations, followed by a brief run of three missions

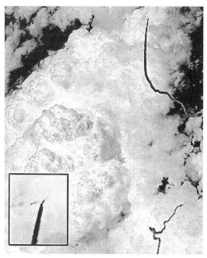

Maj 'Spike' Chuang Jen-Liang flew a hazardous mission over Yunnan Province on 14 May 1966 from Takhli RTAFB. Near Kunming, two SA-2 sites detected him. While his System 13 jammer began to operate, his System 12 alerted him to the launch of three SA-2s. He made the standard 30-degree 'OS' turn, and the missiles wandered away – their smoky trails (seen here in black) were caught by Chuang's tracking camera. He made the first flight to the Lop Nor atomic test area in May 1967 (*Public Domain*)

using the oblique Type H camera from December 1967 and increasing reluctance from President Johnson's regime to allow more, even by SR-71s. A final mission in March 1968, in which the U-2 flown by Capt 'Andy' Fan Hung-Ti was almost intercepted by a MiG-21, ended the 'Black Cats'' direct overflights of China.

Some *Church Door* missions resumed in 1968, when ten were flown by RoCAF Det H pilots alongside two by Det G Americans, and there was another loss when Lt Col 'Billy' Chang Hseih's U-2G 56-6718 disappeared into the Yellow Sea. In 1969 the mission frequency was scaled back, and during the summer of that year the 67th RTS processed only four mission consignments, reducing to one per month in 1970. Some of the copious amounts of U-2 film from each mission, particularly from the aircraft's T70 tracker camera output, was processed in Taiwan, assisted by Eastman Kodak technicians.

Two U-2Rs were delivered to Det H in February 1969, by which time only one U-2C remained in service at Taoyuan. U-2R missions began on 8 April 1969, using the Type H camera, but they were offshore, peripheral flights using oblique cameras and ELINT or System 17 SIGINT receivers from outside Chinese airspace to study the frequencies used by the Red Flag SAM. For U-2Rs on SAC missions, the Type H camera was replaced by the IRIS II panoramic camera in 1969 as it was easier to use. Interception attempts by Chinese J-7s (license-built MiG-21Fs) continued. Several U-2Rs, including 68-10329, were used by Det H from March 1971.

In May 1971, the U-2Rs had the *Long Shaft* COMINT microwave sensor fitted to eavesdrop on communications between Chinese government departments. However, two months later, US relations with Taiwan were about to change in the wake of the visit to Peking by President Richard Nixon's National Security Advisor, Dr Henry Kissinger. Whilst there, he agreed that Taiwan was part of China, and that it should be expelled from the UN. Nevertheless, Det H's two U-2Rs continued with a few missions, most with *Long Shaft* aboard.

'Black Cats' missions ended on 24 May 1974 with a flight over the Yellow Sea by Maj 'Mike' Chiu Song-Chou. The squadron's two CIA U-2Rs were then passed on to the 100th SRW, whilst its processing and support equipment went to the RoCAF, ending *Idealist/Tackle* operations after 14 eventful years. The 'Black Cats' had flown 220 missions across or around China, losing 12 of 28 pilots in accidents or shoot-downs.

The 'Black Cats' tradition survived in the tail markings of the U-2Rs assigned to Det 2 of the 5th SRS/9th SRW at Osan. Equipped with an ASARS-2 nose, 80-1089 was delivered new to the 9th SRW in 1988. The aircraft subsequently flew many orbits along the Korean demilitarized zone prior to being converted into a U-2S in 1995 (*Author's Collection*)

CHAPTER SIX

VIETNAM OPERATIONS

After the cessation of Soviet overflights, the CIA continued to run U-2 operations over Vietnam, Cuba, China and areas of Southeast Asia under the general heading of Project *Idealist*. The collapse of Prince Souvanna Phouma's government in Laos, followed by increased insurgency from the communist Pathet Lao, required seven CIA-sanctioned U-2 flights in 1960 from Clark to survey the ground situation and the rapid build-up of Soviet and North Vietnamese military hardware. Det G U-2As also operated from Cubi Point.

After several 'weather aborts' at the start of January 1961, five Operation *Polecat* missions were undertaken over North Vietnam, Hainan Island and Laos, providing new information on airfields and military bases before the brief TDY ended. Inaccurate maps from the French occupation era could now be corrected with new U-2A mapping imagery following the *Polecat* missions. The 67th RTS Det at Clark processed the film results from early 1961, together with rolls of 35 mm film taken by CIA personnel and others from the US Embassy at Vientiane.

Aerial survey material and cartographic coverage of the area was scarce or outdated, and there were few landmarks for PIs to use as guides for their photo-analysis of jungle-covered territory. In 1960–61, the only U-2 material handled by the 67th RTS labs at Yokota was from overflights of North Vietnam, covering territory from around Vinh up to the Chinese border.

U-2A 56-6690, a serial also attributed to a U-2A that crashed on 19 December 1956 in Arizona, appears on this U-2C, which developed over-speeding problems during a flight over North Vietnam on 8 October 1966 and crashed upon returning to Bien Hoa. The pilot, from the 349th SRS/100th SRW, successfully ejected. It was the only U-2 to be lost on operations during the conflict in Southeast Asia (*Lockheed/Terry Panopalis Collection*)

By 1961, *Able Mabel* 45th TRS RF-101C Voodoo supersonic tactical reconnaissance aircraft were also in-theatre, photographing extensively in Laos and South Vietnam, and using the same overworked 67th RTS facilities as the U-2 detachment. By June 1962 the photo lab had processed 66,430 ft of monochrome film in six months, mostly from long U-2 missions. That figure doubled in January to June 1963, and continued to increase as the lab troops undertook their 12-hour shifts.

Both aircraft types focused on trying to identify and monitor the Ho Chi Minh Trail, with the Voodoos taking on the lower-altitude missions and meeting opposition from the ground. For high-flying U-2s, the results were typically endless high-resolution images of tree-tops. All too often, missions had to be aborted due to heavy cloud and rain obscuring visibility. Also, fragile U-2s had to steer clear of thunderstorms or turbulent air.

In February 1964 the 4080th SRW was ordered to deploy U-2Es 56-6703, 56-6707 and 56-6680 to Clark to supplement the CIA-sponsored pilots' early missions with Det H in Taiwan. These U-2Es were the only ones with inflight refuelling receptacles in their dorsal fairings, which also contained SSB radio equipment. The flight, via Hawaii and supported by KC-135A tankers with the U-2's specialised fuel on board, required two 'shifts' of pilots. Maj Steve Heyser, whose 14 October 1962 mission had revealed the Cuban missiles, was in the first trio.

The first SAC *Lucky Dragon* mission was launched on 13 February, just 24 hours after the U-2s' arrival at Clark, with Maj Jim Qualls being tasked with photographing a North Vietnamese gunboat facility. Cloud obscured the target on this and two subsequent missions (flown by Capts Roger Herman and Jim Rogers). A few days after the det's arrival, political opposition from President Diosdado Macapagal forced its withdrawal from the Philippines on 18 February. The det decamped to Andersen AFB, Guam, which proved to be too far from areas of interest to provide effective reconnaissance coverage.

On 3 March Bien Hoa, in South Vietnam, which was already crowded with numerous USAF and Republic of Vietnam Air Force tactical units, was chosen as OL-20 for the det's three J57-engined U-2Es, albeit for operations in very basic conditions apart from a new 10,000-ft runway. Aircrew lived in trailers and maintainers made do with tents and outdoor showers, although facilities were improved later. There were no available hangars, and U-2s had to be manhandled between tightly packed A-1 Skyraiders into a crude 'nose dock' structure. The first chase car was a 1940s army truck, later replaced by a Ford station wagon. A B-57 squadron arrived from Clark to add to the congestion, closely followed by a squadron of F-100 Super Sabres. A CIA presence with one U-2F also remained at Takhli for *Lazy Daisy* (later, *Lucky Dragon*) missions over selected areas of Laos, the Ho Chi Minh Trail and North Vietnam.

The 4080th's U-2s immediately began some useful mapping work over the whole

56-6707 was one of the first three U-2Es to be sent to Clark in February 1964 to supplement Det H missions from Taiwan. The following month it moved to Bien Hoa. Originally built as Article 374 and delivered to the USAF in May 1957, it is seen here more than a decade later as a black velvet U-2C, together with two unpainted U-2s – CIA aircraft were called 'Articles', with numbers calculated by subtracting 333 from the last three digits of their USAF serials – on the ramp at Palmdale's Plant 42. ECM equipment, including Systems 13/14/15, was installed in modified slipper tanks on the wings' leading edges. *(Lockheed/Terry Panopalis Collection)*

of South Vietnam. Their presence clearly worried the enemy, and it was alleged that the Viet Cong had offered $10,000 bounties for the deaths of any 4080th officers.

Only two or three U-2Es were based at Bien Hoa, partly because it was subjected to frequent Viet Cong rocket attacks, which the U-2s were luckily able to avoid. However, a Quonset hut full of supplies in the high-security area for U-2s and DC-130 Hercules drone launchers was destroyed in one attack. In July 1964 the U-2Es were exchanged for three U-2As.

From the autumn of 1964, the Aircraft Gray-painted U-2s were given an overspray with matt black to reduce their visibility to enemy defences, the grey finish being easily seen by interceptor pilots in trials. Their conspicuous vapour trail at altitude was harder to disguise. The CIA's more powerful J75-engined U-2Cs could climb above the flight level where trails were formed, but SAC U-2As could only reach those altitudes by reducing their fuel loads.

Intensive daily missions continued from Bien Hoa, weather permitting, while Takhli's air-refuellable U-2F performed around three sorties per week. SAC soon took over all the flights in the area, leaving Det G to undertake its final mission on 24 April 1964 before returning to Cubi Point. OL-20 had around 50 personnel, including four pilots, on TDY assignments. Photo processing was initially undertaken at Tan Son Nhut, in South Vietnam, while SIGINT tapes were flown to SAC HQ at Offutt AFB.

Lack of space in the U-2 prevented the installation of TACAN, as used by other military aircraft, so pilots had to rely on the radio compass, celestial navigation and the ground view provided by the periscopic drift sight, or viewfinder, under the nose. Ground Control Approach was available at Bien Hoa to assist with instrument landings in poor visibility. SAC's worldwide high-frequency radio network was used by pilots to send check-in signals during their missions or receive recall messages.

No longer required in Southeast Asia, Det G's U-2F (56-6675) was reassigned to a new Project *Idealist* seven-day deployment at Charbatia, in India. The team was sent in the hope of establishing an OL, but the base was found to be very dilapidated and lacking basic facilities. Despite continued political opposition, preparations were complete in time for a 24 May 1964 mission over Tibet that revealed the build-up of Chinese forces on the border was less than expected. Sadly, the U-2F's brakes failed on landing and it ran off the end of the dirt runway, collapsing the main undercarriage. Pilot Bob Ericson was uninjured, the film was intact and more flights were planned into China, but the aircraft required major repairs and no replacements were available. The deployment was abandoned and the U-2F was airlifted out. Only four missions were flown from Charbatia as a forward staging area until 1967.

SAC U-2 operations over Southeast Asia were code-named *Talent*. The label changed again to *Trojan Horse* in the summer of 1964 and a few missions were called *Cold Tale*. *Lightning Bug* drone reconnaissance sorties, launched from Bien Hoa-based DC-130 Hercules aircraft, were dubbed *China Bumble Bug* (later, *Buffalo Hunter* from Bien Hoa) or *Blue Springs* for 1964 flights over China and North Vietnam. Bien Hoa provided at least

The tiny cockpit of early U-2s was a typically cluttered 1950s 'pit', with the exception of the bomber-type control yoke that was needed to grapple with the aircraft's unpowered flying controls. The drift sight screen with low-glare 'boot' is above the main panel. The throttle (with black vernier control wheel for refined throttle control at altitude), gust control switch and navigation items are on the left below the caged cooling fan (*USAF*)

one *Trojan Horse* sortie daily, usually over North Vietnam. A shortage of aircraft was a constant problem, with only 11 available for all SAC missions and CIA requirements siphoning off several others.

Several CIA Det G missions were flown over Cambodia from Taoyuan in 1964 and in October–November 1965, with occasional missions in February 1966. The last Det G mission from Takhli, by Robert Hall in U-2G 56-6718, occurred on 3 April 1968 and revealed 'no significant military intelligence'. Det G became the 1130th Aerospace Technical Development and Training Group in 1969, moving its focus to the SR-71, but also managing U-2s that took part in aircraft carrier suitability trials.

In December 1967, the 67th RTS at Yokota (where it remained until March 1971) assumed initial processing and 'exploitation' of U-2 imagery, meaning distribution of photographic data to relevant commanders after initial examination by PIs. Photo footage was crucial to all military activity throughout the war, and the quality of high-resolution original negatives from the U-2's advanced camera systems is often still valued above imagery captured by electronic means.

Following the CIA-inspired flights by Det G from Takhli in 1959–60 to investigate China's nuclear research facilities, U-2 overflights of North Vietnam and beyond were well established by 1961. One mission covered the Red River from Hanoi to the Chinese border, concentrating on railway bridges up to Lao Ky, where they connected with a rail line to China. Another late-1961 flight near Vinh showed long truck convoys returning from South Vietnam. Other 1961 missions revealed the new industrial/military complex at Viet Tri, on the main Hanoi rail route. North Vietnam's three operational airfields, Cat Bai, Gia Lam and Phuc Yen (with its newly laid, 9200-ft jet-capable runway and dispersals) were also closely surveyed.

Throughout 1961–62, flights focused increasingly on the Hanoi-Haiphong area, well above any potential threat from the ground. A 21 February 1962 flight over North Vietnam and Chinese-occupied Hainan Island was made from Taoyuan, with US pilot Bob Ericson aboard.

However, the CIA's main focus in seeking to curtail the spread of communism in 1962 resulted in U-2 overflights of Tibet, Kashmir and China's borders with India. U-2F 56-6675, with in-flight refuelling, was used for these extremely long-range sorties from Takhli – its two missions in December 1962 each lasted for 12 hours. Despite welcoming Det G's intelligence input concerning the communist threat to his country, Indian Prime Minister Jawaharlal Nehru publicly resisted the idea of a U-2 OL in India to replace the Peshawar deployments to Pakistan, ruled out after the loss of Frank Powers' U-2.

Ever-increasing reconnaissance demands made a new SAC-operated U-2 data processing centre necessary, and the 13th RTS was established at Tan Son Nhut in April 1963 to relieve pressure on the 67th RTS. However, as a USAF historian noted, 'The U-2 aircraft from Bien Hoa flew very high-altitude photo missions over Southeast Asia. Film from these flights swamped the 13th RTS, which had to call upon other PACAF, SAC and Navy facilities in the Philippines and Japan'.

In fact, the three aircraft in-theatre photographed all of North Vietnam and most of South Vietnam, Cambodia, Thailand and parts of China within a month. The 67th RTS 'techs' coped with much of it, and their

usual eyestrain headaches were about to be worsened by the arrival at Yokota of the 18th TFW's deafening F-105 Thunderchiefs. However, their equipment worked well, with the detachment flying 33 Type B camera sorties before any of them developed a fault.

On 24 July 1965 North Vietnam's SA-2 missile sites claimed their first victim in the form of a 15th TFW F-4C Phantom II, and the U-2's unchallenged reign in North Vietnamese skies suddenly ended. Missions were restricted to South Vietnam and Laos, leaving tactical reconnaissance aircraft to provide intel on North Vietnam's military situation. The loss of high-quality U-2 imagery was a considerable blow to the US war effort, particularly as the Operation *Rolling Thunder* air campaign against North Vietnam was to continue until November 1968. The early Corona satellite imagery lacked fine detail of SAM sites and fighters on airfields. However, acquiring imagery of sufficient quality placed a U-2 within SA-2 range.

North Vietnam's SAM belt was concentrated around Hanoi and Haiphong, with its range extending from the Chinese border to out over the Gulf of Tonkin. U-2s had to enter their target areas along a narrow corridor that ran along the Chinese 'buffer' border zone from the west in order to stay out of range of the SAMs.

Following the appearance of SA-2s in North Vietnam, U-2s were quickly tasked with contributing to a 'complete analysis of the suspect SAM sites', leading to a full report in August 1965. U-2 flights over North Vietnam continued, but they were routed around known SAM sites, although these could be moved to ambush positions elsewhere. The latter made mission planning difficult, and the enemy's skill in camouflaging often frustrated attempts to photograph them. An early Hycon HR-329 Type H camera, capable of taking images at a 70-degree oblique angle, was shipped to OL-20 so that U-2s could avoid overflying known SAM sites, but it proved to be unreliable.

Sanders ECM pods and System 12 offered some protection, but SAM sites proliferated. Capt Ed Purdue, veteran of several risky missions around the Siberian coast in 1962, narrowly avoided an SA-2 over Haiphong in October 1965, having received no warning of its approach. He had

U-2A 56-6951 proved to be too long for the photographer's lens as it taxied past Republic of Vietnam Air Force A-1 Skyraiders and USAF B-57 Canberras at a packed Bien Hoa in 1965. This aircraft was one of five extra U-2s acquired in 1958, and it was eventually lost in a non-fatal accident at Davis-Monthan on 17 October 1966. Black paint was applied in 1964 to counter the threat of interception by North Vietnamese MiGs (USAF/Terry Panopalis collection) reported being under missile attack near Hanoi as early as September 1964. At that time U-2s had no RWR equipment, but Purdue made a planned turn at altitude and saw the missile pass close to him.

SA-2 operators could resort to optical guidance against relatively slow-moving targets like a U-2, assisted by the aircraft's conspicuous condensation trail. Conversion of the 11 SAC U-2As to U-2C configuration, with the J75 engine and larger air intakes, added to the safety element thanks to the later model's increased altitude and contrail elimination. The conversion programme began at Lockheed's secret 'Skunk Works' in October 1965, and revised U-2Cs were delivered to OL-20 from April 1966. The shortage of operational aircraft during this process was a handicap.

The first SAC U-2 write-off in Vietnam was actually a non-combat loss. U-2C 56-6690 was returning to Bien Hoa from an 8 October 1966 mission when Maj Leo Stewart (the operations officer) lost control and bailed out at 46,000 ft. He was rescued, but the U-2's tail section, containing the top-secret System 13 package, fell off and landed in enemy territory 50 miles from Bien Hoa. The system's self-destruct component had not been connected up due to lack of technical data for the maintainers. A 17-man team from the 5th Special Forces Group with Montagnard guides spent four days searching for it in dense jungle before eventually recovering the package intact from deep mud in Operation *Black Box*.

Despite the reduction in U-2 numbers to only 14 in SAC and CIA use, the film processing workload continued to increase. During one five-day period in 1966, more than 400 film batches from seven missions – mainly *Trojan Horse* and *Blue Spring* – were 'reported' (processed and analysed) by one RTS.

From January to May 1967, 67 U-2 missions were flown, 37 of them over North Vietnam, but the increasing SAM threat was making overflights of the Hanoi–Haiphong area too dangerous. Tactical reconnaissance aircraft and drones could provide film from much lower altitudes, but this meant narrower area coverage for IPs searching for new SAM sites. U-2s were forbidden to overfly the 20-mile buffer zone between China and North Vietnam, where substantial defences were located.

At high altitudes above 60,000 ft, drones were as vulnerable to SAMs as U-2s – only five of the 12 high-altitude drones launched over North Vietnam in early 1967 were recovered. Some were ELINT-equipped to try and record the frequencies used in the SA-2 launch procedure. A February 1966 drone sortie sent back the missile's crucial proximity fusing signal, enabling ECM adjustments to jam it. Others 'faked' U-2 flight paths and radar signatures to 'bring up' enemy radar signals for analysis.

Planning the photo analysis of U-2 and RF-4C Phantom II missions to ensure the most effective use of their imagery was assisted from 1965 by the introduction of the time-saving Route Search method that used a massive IBM 1401 computer and precise calculation to predict where targets would show up on the photographs. From December 1967, the 67th RTS handled only the initial phases of *Giant Dragon* 'exploitation' of U-2R imagery, before passing the task on to the 548th RTS in July 1969.

When the U-2 was effectively forced out of North Vietnam by the proliferation of SAM sites and Washington's reluctance to attack them, the U-2's complex, time-consuming Type B camera footage had less priority. The aircraft was confined to missions over lower threat areas of Cambodia, parts of North Vietnam and the Ho Chi Minh Trail areas of South Vietnam bordering Laos, as well as occasional *Church Door* flights for the RoCAF. There were also specifically CIA-requested operations across the areas of northern Laos bordering China, where, in 1965, a new road joining the two countries was detected – it was thought that China might enter the war in Laos directly.

Having overcome fears of provoking China and the CIA's Japanese hosts, U-2 missions over North Vietnam were largely replaced by CIA A-12 *Black Shield* or 'BX' Mach 3 flights above 80,000 ft. From May 1967 they covered most of the North Vietnam missions. A-12s and U-2s, although extremely costly to obtain, were still much cheaper than using satellites. A-12 missions from Det 1 at Kadena, on Okinawa, began soon after the first three arrived in May 1967 for a one-year deployment. Their missions were planned so that they did not overlap coverage from U-2 flights. However, the A-12s were returned to the USA during 1968 and stored as part of the shrinkage of Project *Idealist*. *Black Shield* missions were subsequently performed by USAF SR-71As of the 9th SRW.

In 1969 the CIA's U-2R operations were to be transferred to SAC, although Henry Kissinger managed to reverse this decision and maintain a CIA U-2 programme. He argued that keeping a U-2R detachment in Taiwan enabled overflights of China without direct political risk to the US government and preserved good relations with the Chinese Nationalists.

Introduction of the improved U-2R to Southeast Asia was initially resisted by Washington because it was felt that North Vietnam's defences would soon include more capable missiles such as the SA-5 and possibly new generation, high-altitude interceptors like the MiG-25. In fact, Moscow did not significantly upgrade the North's air defences during the war.

Giant Dragon flights were eventually made by OL-20 U-2Rs, two of which were at Bien Hoa by July 1969 for missions over Cambodia and Laos. North Vietnamese air defences had gradually moved into those areas to protect parts of the Ho Chi Minh Trail, so escort by F-105F *Wild Weasel* anti-SAM aircraft and F-4D/E fighters was required. The extra effort was worthwhile, as the U-2 imagery was extremely revealing in showing camouflaged trucks and the effects of air strikes on the Trail's vehicular traffic, even including bicycles. It was also used by SAC to make mosaic images of ground areas that became bombing 'boxes' for B-52 *Arc Light* strikes. After a strip of terrain had been blown apart by a B-52 cell – 324 500-lb bombs – the interpreters could count how many of them had fallen within the 'boxes'.

U-2 flights from Bien Hoa over North Vietnam ended in June 1970 as part of the general drawdown of forces. The detachment moved with its single U-2R to the B-52 base at U-Tapao as OL-RU to fly *Giant Nail* photo missions over Laos and Cambodia. From 1970 the aircraft was also involved in innovative trials of data-linked COMINT equipment, collecting and recording information on enemy transmissions and beaming it automatically from over the Gulf of Tonkin to a ground station at Nakhon Phanom, in Thailand.

After further tests, operational sorties known as *Senior Book* began, providing regular SIGINT on activity in North Vietnam and areas of China from a range of 300 miles. Intelligence data became accessible much faster than when only wet photograph processing was available, but as Maj Bob Uebelacker

U-2R 68-10340 of the 100th SRW taxies in at Bien Hoa after a 1969 mission. This aircraft was lost following a sortie over the Korean demilitarized zone on 5 October 1980, 68-10340 crashing at Osan – Capt Cleveland Wallace successfully ejected. U-2R/Ss could only operate from reinforced runways and taxiways due to the aircraft's extra weight being focused on one main undercarriage unit (*Terry Panopalis Collection*)

commented in 1987, 'In Vietnam it took four hours or so to get the data to the battle commanders. Today, all of USAFE works in near real time'.

A third U-2R was sent to U-Tapao, and they alternated *Giant Nail* photo sorties with *Senior Book* (*Olympic Torch* from April 1972) COMINT. Pilots and maintenance crews served 90-day tours. During 1971–72, they provided timely information on North Vietnam's air defences from their high-altitude 'perch' via a KC-135 radio relay aircraft. Missions usually involved tedious orbits, which were so useful in providing data on the state of North Vietnam's missile launches and its reserves of SA-2s that the 100th SRW received the Paul T Cullen Memorial Award for 'outstanding' and 'unique' contributions to Operation *Linebacker II* and the war in general.

Links with the *Teaball* Weapons Control Center at Nakhon Phanom enabled warning of SAM radar activity, SA-2 launches and MiG threats to be relayed to B-52 and tactical aircraft crews. There were also links to US Navy *Red Crown* radar ships offshore. A U-2R pilot would be able to watch SAMs being launched at the US strikers, call out warnings and monitor the numbers of missiles fired. Imagery from U-2s and other reconnaissance platforms of bomb damage to North Vietnamese targets after each *Linebacker* attack was a priority for SAC and Washington planners.

The change of emphasis and increased importance for the U-2Rs prompted the conversion of the U-Tapao Det into a full squadron – the 99th SRS, initially commanded by Col Buddy Brown. It also controlled *Buffalo Hunter* drones that continued their photographic flights over North Vietnam. Missions continued after the cease-fire in January 1973, and the U-2Rs were modified with larger pods on their wing leading edges for more ambitious Melpar-designed COMINT packages. New blade antennas were added below the pods and the revised equipment became operational in 1974 in the *Senior Spear* programme.

When Hanoi's invasion of South Vietnam seemed imminent in 1974, a fourth U-2R went to U-Tapao to enable two sorties to be flown daily. One of the 99th SRS's tasks was to monitor the seizure of the US intelligence vessel *Mayaguez* by the Khmer Rouge in Cambodia, acting as an airborne communications centre for the forces sent to rescue its crew. A few COMINT and *Olympic Meet* photographic missions continued into 1975, but under pressure from the Thai government, the 99th SRS withdrew after its final *Olympic Torch* mission on 15 March 1976. The unit set up shop with other 100th SRW assets at Osan to provide long-term COMINT surveillance of North Korea in *Olympic Game* missions from 26 February 1976. Two aircraft were made available from July.

CHAPTER SEVEN

NEW VARIANTS

Attrition had almost halved the original U-2 force of 55 aircraft by 1963, and the 'Dragon Lady' had proved so useful that Kelly Johnson realised new production was a possibility. Constructing an improved version was complicated by Lockheed's commitment to Project *Oxcart*, with fighter and reconnaissance versions of the Mach 3+-capable A-12 being sponsored by the CIA and USAF, and by the latter's preference for the wide-winged RB-57F, with increased capacity for reconnaissance equipment but inferior maximum altitude to the U-2.

Nevertheless, the 'Skunk Works' designers outlined the U-2L, with a longer fuselage and aircraft carrier capability to increase the number of potential 'bases' beyond the relatively scarce land options. A U-2M, equipped with either a large telescope or an Itek 240-inch focal length camera to observe Soviet satellites or ground targets, was also proposed. Further studies of new wing designs were undertaken in 1965, and the development of the Pratt & Whitney's J75-P-13B with 17,000 lbs of thrust offered improved rates of climb and restoration of the 75,000-ft high-altitude performance. Revised air intakes were needed to make the most of the uprated engine.

In October 1965 Johnson instructed designer Merv Heal to undertake a full revision of the U-2. By January 1966, the U-2R ('R' for 'revised') had evolved under CIA sponsorship in the absence of interest from the USAF. The design proposed by veteran Lockheed engineer Ed Baldwin

On 28 August 1967, the very first U-2R (68-10329), with Lockheed test pilot Bill Park at the controls, undertook its maiden flight. All of the CIA's U-2s operated out of the Edwards North Base complex, and the R-model's flight testing also took place from here (*James C Goodall Collection*)

had a 103-ft wingspan (23 ft wider than the U-2A) and a fuselage 13 ft 4 in longer than early models.

Although maximum take-off weight increased to 37,585 lbs, compared with 19,665 lbs for the U-2A, there were welcome improvements in performance. In a U-2R, cruise speed was usually set at Mach 0.72 (160 knots indicated air speed at high altitude, but equivalent to 420 knots true airspeed). A slow, steady climb was sustained for most missions on the basis that the aircraft would continue to gain height until it was required to descend, or when it ran out of fuel. Uniquely, throughout the climb the pilot had to progressively reduce the throttle setting, and operating the throttle at all at 70,000 ft could risk a flame-out.

With increased fuel capacity and new tank arrangements, a U-2R's endurance of 15 hours was five hours longer than a U-2A's, adding 2300 miles to the range. It could reach 75,500 ft, 1500 ft more than a U-2C, with the same engine. From the outset, the re-design included provision for interchangeable, elongated nose sections which would massively increase the versatility of these second-generation U-2s and expand their payloads to around 4000 lbs.

Approval for the U-2R by the end of 1966 came none too soon, as only 15 short-winged aircraft remained available. The addition of four extra U-2Rs to the original CIA order for eight in January 1967 for Project *Idealist* was based partly on evidence of the aircraft's improved survivability against SAMs and other threats, including the MiG-21. Further enhancements included a 45 per cent larger cockpit to allow pilots use of the new David Clark S1010-B pressure suit (regulation wear above 50,000 ft), an all-moving tailplane, a longer tailpipe to reduce the engine's IR signature, a zero–zero ejection seat and the inclusion of Doppler radar, ILS and TACAN as standard equipment, together with a VHF radio. An

Bill Park, wearing an AP22S flight suit, prepares to take the first U-2R aloft on 9 September 1967, 12 days after its first flight (*Lockheed/Terry Panopalis Collection*)

LN-33 inertial navigation system (INS) known as Igor made traditional celestial navigation unnecessary. A liquid oxygen bottle replaced the pressurised gaseous oxygen spheres of earlier U-2s, extending the aircraft's endurance.

Two sets of hydraulically assisted spoilers were fitted above the wings – an inner set to be raised at 60 degrees below 105 knots in the descent phase of flight, and an outer set for roll control assistance at low altitudes. However, the cable-operated main flying controls of earlier models were retained.

The first aircraft (68-10329) was ready for Bill Park to undertake its maiden flight on 28 August 1967. The flight test team at that time included Frank Powers, although he did not fly the U-2R. Despite the aircraft being slightly less sensitive to the high-altitude 'stall margin' than earlier models, it still lacked powered controls to save weight. The unique bicycle landing gear was also retained.

Basic U-2 flying characteristics remained unchanged, as did the bomber-sized control yoke. The aircraft was renowned for providing pilots with the highest workload of any military type they flew. According to Col Gaines, this was particularly arduous 'during the take-off and landing phases, and basically any time you were hand-flying the aircraft, due to the U-2's instability and tendency to wander off course or altitude. Any bank angle caused the fuel in the wing on the "down" side to run to the tip and exacerbate the bank. Correcting this with the ailerons, which were each about ten feet long, would cause more than average adverse yaw as well.

'The control forces were heavy! That was probably the single most surprising and shocking thing I noticed on my "interview" ride. The instant I put my hands on the control yoke I realised the U-2 was unlike anything I had flown before. A two-hour "pattern" sortie was exhausting. The U-2 had a yoke for a reason, and rolling in and out of turns low down was a two-handed task.'

SEA DRAGONS

The loss of Frank Powers' U-2 produced a political backlash that severely limited the number of countries that would covertly or openly host U-2 detachments. An alternative, proposed by Kelly Johnson in 1957, was to use aircraft carriers as mobile bases. The idea was rejected by the USAF at that stage, but by March 1963 it had become more attractive, and Johnson offered three U-2s with tailhooks, beefed-up undercarriages and fuel dumping vents in case of emergency carrier landings – a useful modification that was added to all U-2s. There were clearly disadvantages involved in the concept apart from the extra 300 lbs of weight associated with these additions, not least the potential compromising of U-2 secrecy and the difficulty of handling the aircraft for carrier landings and launches.

On 4 August 1963, CIA U-2C 56-6685/'N315X', marked as belonging to the 'Office for Naval Research' but unmodified for carrier operations, was loaded onto USS *Kitty Hawk* (CVA-63) at NAS North Island, San Diego, and manoeuvred into the hangar deck via a lift using a 'Low Boy' castoring trolley. The next day, test pilot Bob Schumacher took off into a 30-knot wind, using 321 ft of flightdeck. Pogo wheels were omitted to save potential damage when they were shed, and instead the wingtips were held level by deck crew while Schumacher wound up the J75 engine. He made three deck approaches and a touch-and-go landing before returning to the 'Skunk Works'.

Two ex-USAF U-2As (56-6681 and 56-6695) were transferred for carrier conversion as U-2Gs, including the fitment of J75 engines, in Project *Whale Tale*. Spoilers were added to the wings and the flap extension angle was increased to facilitate landing in the correct place to catch an arrestor cable, rather than 'floating' over the deck as U-2s tended to do on runways.

Col Bill Gregory, Det G commander, and his pilots undertook carrier qualifications in US Navy jet trainers early in 1964, and in February of that year trials resumed aboard USS *Ranger* (CVA-61). Turbulence from the carrier became a problem as the U-2Gs made their flat, level landing

The first five U-2Rs built by Lockheed sit side by side on the ramp at the CIA's operating facility at the Edwards North Base complex in mid-1968. In the foreground is unpainted prototype 68-10329, wearing its civilian registration 'N803X' on the fin. The aircraft was reworked to production standard and delivered to the Agency in March 1969 (*James C Goodall Collection*) approaches, the aircraft sometimes drifting to within ten feet of the ship's superstructure. A small pogo wheel was added under the aircraft's nose to prevent damage after a U-2 bounced during one landing, damaging the nose. *Ranger*'s speed was reduced to cut down turbulence. The wingtip skids were reinforced after another landing almost ended in a crash.

Once the CIA pilots had become carrier qualified, the U-2G was used for its only carrier-based operational mission, codenamed *Fish Hawk*, in May 1964. *Ranger* sailed to the South Atlantic so that a U-2G could secretly photograph the new French nuclear test site on Mururoa Atoll, in French Polynesia. A second mission was disapproved by the US Navy and cancelled, as were proposed flights over areas of interest in the Middle East from a Sixth Fleet carrier. One U-2G (56-6715) was lost during carrier landing practice at Edwards on 26 April 1965 due to fuel imbalance in the wing tanks, killing experienced Det G pilot Eugene 'Buster' Edens. The fuel transfer valves were then modified and retractable stall strips added to the wing leading edges to improve stability when landing.

Kelly Johnson realised that he would only break even on the order for 12 U-2Rs (eight of which would be lost in accidents, four of them fatal), so he sought US Navy approval for the aircraft to act as a high-altitude communications relay platform for carrier task groups. Two U-2Rs (including 'N812X') were modified with the U-2G tailhook and flaps that could be lowered to a 50-degree angle, as well as manually foldable outer wing panels that reduced the wingspan by 12 ft for carrier deck handling. This modification was applied to all U-2Rs so that they could fit most USAF hangars.

Bill Park and four Det G pilots, including two from the RAF, undertook carrier qualification trials on board USS *America* (CVA-66) in November 1969 during Project *Blue Gull V*. The trials were supervised by USAF Operations Officer Maj Dan Schmarr. *Blue Gull V* landings were less challenging than the *Whale Tale* events, and the carrier's crew were impressed by the U-2R's short take-off distance from the flightdeck without a catapult. Det G pilots were soon ready for operational flights, but US Navy reservations about the cost-effectiveness of devoting a carrier, with part of its Carrier Air Wing removed to make way for a U-2, to a voyage that might focus on only one U-2 mission curtailed the programme.

Kelly Johnson kept the US Navy in his sights, nevertheless, proposing the U-2R as a land-based electronic patrol/ocean surveillance aircraft, for which it was evaluated in Project *Highboy* (Electronic Patrol Experimental – EP-X), and later as an anti-shipping platform, carrying four Condor long-range missiles. U-2R 68-10399 was used for *Highboy*, with a large weather radar in its nose and wing pods containing an ALQ-110 ELINT sensor and a video camera. Data link and astro-tracking were included. Flight tests in 1973, in which all sensors were controlled by a ground station rather than the pilot, were productive and

U-2G 'N808X', with Bob Schumacher at the controls, catches the third wire as the aircraft lands on board *Ranger* on 29 February 1964 on its second attempt. The U-2 bounced just as the tailhook caught the arresting wire, pitching the aircraft forward and slamming its nose into the flightdeck (*Lockheed Martin/Terry Panopalis Collection*)

there was strong interest from elements in
the US Navy for EP-X as a long-duration
alternative to the US Navy's P-3 Orion.
However, by late 1974 (and the end of
Johnson's career), it was clear that powerful
voices in favour of satellites and the usual
fears that foreign bases would be unavailable
ruled out further EP-X progress.

The U-2R had proved its worth, but
it was soon apparent that the order for
only 12 had been inadequate. Attrition
had made a supplementary order for five
more U-2As necessary in 1958, and by
the late 1970s further attrition meant that
the tiny numbers of U-2R survivors were being severely overworked.
Alternatives in the form of the Ryan *Compass Arrow* or Boeing *Compass
Cope* unmanned reconnaissance drones were not sufficiently developed.
Kelly Johnson even proposed a remotely piloted 'U-2 RPV' as a
way of securing more orders and producing a cheaper vehicle than
Compass Cope.

U-2R 68-10333, sporting civil registration
'N812X', has just landed back on board
America during Project *Blue Gull V* carrier
suitability trials, which were undertaken off
the Virginia Capes between 21–23
November 1969 (*US Navy*)

The long-standing need for more U-2s was finally addressed in 1978
when an order for 25 TR-1s – a 'new version of the U-2' – was announced
for tactical reconnaissance ('TR'). The massive increase in Warsaw Pact
armament, considerably outnumbering NATO forces, led planners to seek
improved intelligence-gathering methods. The U-2R was the basis of the
new order, renamed to 'get this spyplane label off the aircraft', as the
chairman of the Joint Chiefs of Staff, Gen David Jones, wished. The legacy
of the 1960 Powers shoot-down had to be finally expunged by a new label.

The tooling, most of which Johnson had carefully preserved despite
orders to destroy it, generally remained the same, except that the external
stiffeners added to the horizontal stabilisers of U-2Rs to reduce fatigue
caused by engine vibration were replaced by stiffer internal structures.
J75-P-13B engines were refurbished from retired F-105 Thunderchiefs
and F-106 Delta Darts. Externally, small wingtip pods for a new Dalmo
Victor System 27 RWR were added, and these were also retro-fitted to
the surviving U-2Rs. The RWR was controlled via a new cockpit threat
warning panel.

The US Navy evaluated the U-2R as a land-
based electronic patrol/ocean surveillance
aircraft in Project *Highboy* (EP-X). Highly
modified U-2R 68-10339 undertook the
trials, the aircraft featuring a large weather
radar in its nose and wing pods containing
an ALQ-110 ELINT sensor and a video
camera. Flight testing commenced in 1973
(Lockheed Martin)

The two TR-1B trainers were delivered to the 9th SRW in early 1983 at the beginning of the aircraft's production run. Both 'Two-headed Goats' were later converted to TU-2S configuration and re-finished in black in 1984–85 (*Author's Collection*)

NASA's U-2C 56-6681 at Ames Research Center at Moffett Field in January 1977 with a selection of the Q-bay loads available for its Earth Survey work. This aircraft was retired in August 1987 following 16 years of service with NASA – by then it had logged more than 10,000 hours. It has been on display at the Ames facility for more than 30 years (*NASA/Terry Panopalis Collection*)

Site 7 at Palmdale's Air Force Plant 42 was reactivated and the stored tooling refurbished 12 years after U-2R production had ended in 1969. It took time to assemble a suitably skilled work force, including some retired U-2R workers, and production had a slow start. An initial contract covered two USAF TR-1As in 1979, with the intention of purchasing a total of 35. In fact, 37 were manufactured. Seven were originally intended for Taiwan as more capable U-2Rs, but the changing political situation resulted in them entering USAF service. The batch included two TR-1B two-seaters (80-1064 and -1065). A single U-2R(T) trainer (80-1091) was also included.

The first TR-1A flew on 1 August 1981, and deliveries to the 9th SRW began in September. The usual competition over 'ownership' arose, this time between SAC and Tactical Air Command (TAC), rather than SAC and the CIA. In a compromise solution, SAC took over the aircraft but TAC, through USAFE (where the TR-1As would be deployed), had responsibility for using them, providing targets and ground stations.

The TR-1 production order also included two ER-2s ('ER' for 'Earth Resources') for NASA's High-Altitude Aircraft Program, begun in 1971 with a pair of loaned SAC U-2Cs that were finally retired in 1989. The first off the line was ER-2 80-1063, delivered to NASA in June 1981. The ER-2s, which were TR-1As with USAF equipment such as defensive electronics replaced by research payloads, could still carry the TR-1's sensor systems if necessary. The second aircraft was delivered in 1989, and NASA's Ames Research Center at Moffett Field, California, also leased a third ex-9th SRW TR-1A (80-1069).

Research programmes undertaken by the aircraft have included investigation of clear air turbulence, storm research in Project *Rough Rider* and frequent surveys of natural disasters resulting from fires, earthquakes and volcanic activity. Air sampling of pollutants and ozone layer research have also been carried out.

SAC U-2Rs

In 1968 the USAF decided that it too needed U-2Rs to replace its handful of surviving 'short wing' airframes, which had become so heavy with additional equipment that the difference between stall buffet speed and excess speed, both leading to possible structural failure at high altitude, had been reduced to around six knots, requiring constant vigilance by the pilot. Anything beyond a shallow 12-degree banking turn would reduce the margin further, placing the pilot in what was dubbed 'coffin corner'. Some aircraft, which had flown up to 4000 hours, were also manifesting metal fatigue and corrosion, requiring major refurbishment.

Under pressure from SAC, Robert S McNamara tried to commandeer all 12 contracted U-2Rs for the USAF's 100th SRW, but it finally had to settle for only six, with the rest going to CIA management. The cost of U-2 operations, and the aircraft's increasing vulnerability to enemy defences, brought pressure to cancel it in the early 1980s, notably from the Deputy Director of Defence, Frank Carlucci. It required strenuous Congressional campaigning by Gen Jerome O'Malley, former CO of the 9th SRW, to secure 'life extensions' for the U-2 and SR-71.

Improvements to the U-2R continued during testing. A new Itek IRIS II panoramic camera with a constantly rotating mirror and lens assembly was adopted to replace the Type B camera, the 660-lb Hycon Type H camera and the Itek System 112D twin stereo camera. The first two 100th SRW pilots were checked out in the U-2R via a 20-hour conversion course in July 1968, and the aircraft became operational in January 1969. Several innovative experiments to increase the U-2R's versatility began in 1969 at Edwards AFB, including Project *Fortune Cookie*, which partnered the U-2R with a supersonic reconnaissance drone. Two Beech AQM-37 drones, carried by a Det G U-2R, would be launched towards enemy air defence sites to activate their SAM radars and transmit ELINT data from them back to the U-2R, or other receivers in the area. Political opposition terminated the project before flight tests began.

U-2Rs proved their worth in monitoring the ceasefire agreed in August 1970 when the Middle East conflict flared up over Egypt's attempts to retake areas of Sinai. Det G was allocated the task, hoping to operate from Akrotiri, with two RAF pilots flying the aircraft. At the last minute the British government withdrew approval for the RAF pilots. Instead, Marty Knutson and Bob Ericson, on the final deployment in their long careers on the U-2, had to make the flights, crossing the Atlantic to Upper Heyford and then skirting around France and Italy, which had refused overflight permission. After patrolling the narrow strip of land separating the two armies along the Suez Canal, they recovered to Akrotiri. Throughout the patrol flights, they had to keep to a narrow corridor inside Israeli territory, as neither the Egyptians nor their Soviet support forces had agreed to the flights. Observation flights continued until November, by which time 30 had been flown.

Like their 9th SRW SR-71 stablemates, some U-2R crews abroad adopted individual 'tail art' on their aircraft. U-2R 80-1076 featured this design on 28 August 1988, while U-2R 68-10332 was seen with a Snoopy-with-wine-bottle cartoon while at Akrotiri in a tribute to Cyprus's vineyards (*Terry Panopalis Collection*)

CHAPTER EIGHT

BATTLEFIELD RECONNAISSANCE

ALSS was an early attempt at coordinating ELINT from several U-2Cs to fix and attack SAM sites. U-2C 56-6714 was taken out of storage in 1972 for the project, and it joined four other *Senior Ball* 100th SRW U-2Cs at Wethersfield in May 1975 in a two-tone 'Sabre' grey scheme (*Terry Panopalis Collection*)

The Vietnam War re-emphasised the importance of photo-reconnaissance in providing planners with the relevant data to conduct military operations. Det 2 photo-surveillance over the Suez Canal in 1956 was effectively tactical reconnaissance in support of land action. The conflict in Southeast Asia also saw the growth of various types of electronic intelligence gathering. The U-2 became an increasingly important element in that 'battle of the beams' with enemy radars and communications. The gathering of COMINT assumed increasing importance as command-and-control procedures on the battlefield became more sophisticated. Locating and providing warning of SAM sites and launches was one of the U-2R's key functions in the latter stages of the war.

A constant problem for electronic reconnaissance platforms and aircraft involved in suppression of enemy air defences (SEAD) was that 'Fan Song' radars were only turned on briefly after aircraft targets had already been tracked by other types of radar. This did not allow an SEAD aircraft or U-2 time to fly near the hostile radar site and establish its position with direction-finding electronic equipment. Also, if 'Fan Song' operators realised that an anti-radiation missile had been launched at their radar, they would simply shut down and the missile would fail to track.

After Vietnam, experiments in that area continued. The Advanced Location and Strike System (ALSS) programme involved three U-2s flying above suspected air defence radar sites with their ELINT sensors data-linked to a ground station. By using triangulation, the location of the threat emitter could then be established quickly and SEAD aircraft sent in to attack it. Five early U-2s were equipped with ALSS receivers in their 'Q' bays, together with the current System 12F, 13C and 20 self-defence packages.

Following initial tests on the White Sands Missile Range, in New Mexico, the programme was to be moved to Vietnam for operational evaluation. However, delays and technical problems occurred and fighter-bomber activity in Southeast Asia had been drastically scaled back by mid-1973. Tests showed that the system could work well, locating radar sites to within less than 100 ft, but it was inconsistent across the range of emitter wavelengths.

Further trials were arranged in Europe as part of the USAF's *Pave Strike* programme. The five U-2Cs were flown to RAF Wethersfield, in Essex, for a 90-day deployment, and they flew racetrack orbits along the West German border, feeding data to a ground station at Sembach. USAF F-4 Phantom IIs equipped to receive ALSS data were the strikers. In 18 planned test missions, the results were too inconsistent to adopt the system, although more advanced versions were planned.

ALSS programme aircraft 56-6714 was involved in one of the strangest mishaps in the U-2 saga. On 31 January 1980, Capt Ed Beaumont was flying from Beale AFB when he suffered a catatonic seizure at 14,000 ft, reducing him to virtual unconsciousness, although his finger was locked on the 'transmit' button on his throttle. His aircraft began a gentle descent, pursued by several T-37 trainers. Eventually, the U-2C flew down a narrow valley in mountainous terrain. Its wingtip hit power lines but it flew under them and made a relatively gentle landing in a wet rice field. Beaumont came round, shut down the engine, tried to eject the canopy, which was jammed, and then broke through it with a special canopy breaker tool. As he crawled out through the hole in the glass, he accidentally stepped on his 'un-safed' ejection seat ring, and the seat flung him out into the swampy field. Beaumont survived and his aircraft was later displayed atop a pylon at Beale.

Radar imaging became crucial to the next stage of the U-2's career as it patrolled the Forward Edge of the Battlefield (FEBA) investigating the Warsaw Pact countries' Electronic Order of Battle. APQ-56 sideways-looking radar had been installed in some early U-2s, but the results achieved were greatly inferior to conventional photography. By 1970, solid state circuits could be used to process radar imagery digitally and provide high-resolution ground maps of varied dimensions. U-2R 68-10339 was fitted with a new Goodyear radar for UPD-X – Project *Senior Lance* – in 1971. Its X-band technology enabled the radar to 'see' targets (even camouflaged objects) at a range of 100 miles, day and night, in all weather conditions. Patrols of the Cuban coastline were productive, and the system was enhanced by adding data link in 1972.

9th SRW *Senior Book* U-2R 68-10336 visited Mildenhall in August 1976 for NATO Exercises *Cold Fire* and *Teamwork*, and another spent four months at the airfield in 1977. It flew more than 30 *Olympic Flame* SIGINT missions along the West German border, downloading data to a ground station near Hahn. The impressive results prompted SAC plans to station a permanent U-2 detachment, Det 4, in Britain. A combined ELINT system, tested in U-2R 68-10339, used elements of the *Senior Spear* and *Senior Ruby* systems in the 24-ft long 'superpods' attached to the wings. Fitting these monsters required modification to the trailing edge flaps to allow for the rear section of the pod.

Further tests over West Germany again elicited very positive responses from NATO commanders on how the systems suited the NATO tactical situation in monitoring the numerous Warsaw Pact radar emitters and communications hubs. Additional *Senior Glass* missions were conducted in 1979 by 68-10339 flying over northern Europe and downloading data to a US Navy ship. Similar sorties were flown from Mildenhall in September 1980, with USS *Nimitz* (CVN-68) as the 'ground station'.

The following year, the advent of the TR-1A coincided with the development of two new sensor systems to help US and NATO forces keep track of enemy movements in a potential surprise attack over a wide front. With smaller military resources than a full-scale Soviet assault would present, NATO had to be sure where the enemy's crucial command centres, weapons stores and radar sites were located, together with likely chokepoints in the terrain so that they could be attacked precisely. Advanced Synthetic Aperture Radar System (ASARS) and Precision Emitter Location and Strike System (PELSS) were designed to provide that kind of data quickly and accurately in all weathers.

In 1977 the U-2 received US Army and USAF support as the ideal platform for ASARS, and they wanted control of the system over the battlefield to pass from SAC to the theatre commanders. This decision was a major factor in the re-starting of U-2R/TR-1A production. In common with other SIGINT packages, ASARS-2 was intended to be operated by a ground station. This included the TR-1 Ground Station, or TRIGS, which had not been completed by the end of the Cold War, and the GE/Ferranti TR-1 ASARS Data Manipulation System, which could be manned by RAF personnel. Ford Aerospace's ground station, the TR-1 Exploitation Demonstration System, was also delayed, slowing the operational debut of ASARS.

Hughes Radar Systems Group had developed ASARS, and in August 1981 an ASARS-2 radar was flight-tested in U-2R 68-10336 in an extended nose that contained a phased-array antenna, transmitter and receiver/exciter. Other related electronic packages went into the Q-bay and the datalink boxes were housed in a pressurised compartment behind the rear landing gear. All the components were linked by fibre-optic cables.

The system's main advantage was that it produced imagery outside the visible electromagnetic spectrum, enabling it to 'see' through darkness, cloud and smoke and produce imagery sharp enough to show landmines, small vehicles and metal fences. Backgrounds could be filtered out to isolate objects of interest and a 'change detection' mode could compare an image with a previous one, instantly revealing any differences. This could all be done in real time by a ground station operator viewing the imagery on a screen and relaying information immediately to force commanders.

ASARS-2 became the most capable reconnaissance radar in US aircraft, and it was enhanced by the addition of a Hughes moving target indicator and, in the mid-1990s, by a full improvement programme which increased coverage and refined resolution of its imagery considerably. In Operation *Desert Storm* in early 1991, ASARS-2 would prove to be invaluable when it came to targeting for Coalition strike aircraft. Lt Gen Chuck Horner,

Commander, US Central Command Air Forces, commented, 'With ASARS my aircraft hit the target. Without it, they just hit sand'.

For the pilot, the three-foot ASARS nose extension made little difference to the aircraft's handling, but as Col Gaines observed, 'The biggest issue was lack of visibility over the nose in the flare to land – another good reason to have a mobile [pilot] – but it was easy to get used to'.

PELSS was a less straightforward matter. Ten of the new TR-1A/U-2R production batch had been scheduled to use the system, which had received a lengthy development process beginning with the ALSS-equipped U-2C trials in 1973 and continuing with efforts to find a system that could find and track hostile SAMs and other radars. In practice, it would have needed the same 'triad' of orbiting aircraft, with ELINT-equipped TR-1As replacing U-2Cs to triangulate a radar's position and transmit the data digitally to a ground station. PELSS (later, PLSS) was supposed to cover a huge range of frequencies at ranges of up to 300 nautical miles, and providing 24-hour coverage would have required 12 TR-1As plus spares.

A contract was awarded to the Lockheed Missiles and Space Company in 1977, but the first testbed TR-1A (80-1074) did not begin trials until 1984, complete with a new flat-sided nose for the E-Systems ELINT antenna and receivers and superpods containing the datalink and distance measuring equipment. Further tests by the 9th SRW took place in 1985.

During the long delays, newer systems, including the E-8A Joint STARS aircraft and the IBM AN/APR-38 that equipped F-4G *Wild Weasel* SEAD fighters, became available to perform similar radar detection activities. In the mid-1980s there was some Congressional pressure to put JSTARS, a sophisticated battlefield surveillance and management system sponsored by both the USAF and US Army, into the TR-1. The USAF wanted it in a larger aircraft, so the E-8 was chosen instead. PLSS was cancelled in 1988 after 15 years of development.

In October 1982 the TR-1s were allocated to a new unit in the form of the 95th Reconnaissance Squadron (RS) with SAC's 17th Reconnaissance Wing (RW) at Alconbury, in Cambridgeshire. At the same time Det 4 at Mildenhall ended its U-2R activity to focus on SR-71 operations. The first two TR-1As (80-1068 and 80-1070) arrived in February 1983, welcomed by 17th RW commander Col Tom Lesan, a veteran of Det G operations in the early 1970s. Six TR-1As were in place by March 1985, closely followed by ASARS nose units. The full complement of 12 aircraft and 18 pilots was soon achieved, enabling two jets to be flying orbits over Europe around

Delivered to the 9th TRW in February 1984, TR-1A 80-1074 acted as a testbed for the stillborn PLSS programme. Seen here during a photo-flight over the San Francisco Bay Area in March 1985, the aircraft was eventually issued to the 17th RW at Alconbury in December 1990, before returning to the 9th SRW in October 1992. 80-1074 was converted into a U-2S four years later (*USAF*)

Capt Mark Spencer descends from the cockpit of TR-1A 80-1068 after flying directly from Beale to Alconbury on 1 February 1983. The aircraft, which had been delivered new to the 9th SRW less than seven months earlier, became the first 'Dragon Lady' to join the recently formed 95th RS upon its arrival in Suffolk (*USAF*)

the clock if necessary. Wide-span hangars were constructed at the base to accommodate the TR-1A.

Poor weather conditions were often a challenge, as 95th RS pilot Maj Steve Randle told the author at the time;

'Diversions for weather, particularly due to cross-winds, are something that we get a lot more practice in around here than we would like to. We can use Bedford, but we prefer to go to Lakenheath and Mildenhall, both for proximity and because they have certain ground equipment that is compatible with us. Sometimes we are fortunate to get whatever we can get!'

The first ASARS-2 sortie was flown on 9 July 1985. The new TR-1As proved their worth immediately over the potential battlefields of Europe, gathering SIGINT at a range of up to 350 miles and sending it automatically to the Tactical Ground Intercept Facility in West Germany. ASARS noses were only used for operational missions, and around four TR-1As were normally configured for action. For training (and all missions counted for a training credit), the basic 'slick' nose was used, usually together with superpods. A two-seat TR-1B visited each year to provide two-seat check rides for drivers. As Maj Randle commented in 1987, 'We lack a two-seat airplane here, which makes it fairly hard to evaluate and standardise in-flight performance'.

Shortage of two-seaters was a problem throughout the U-2's service life, but safety steadily improved. The 95th RS sustained only one mishap in its first five years when, in October 1983, a runway contractor's vehicle was left with its handbrake off. Taxiing TR-1A 80-1069 was hit in the wing by the vehicle, causing damage of more than $1m. Although the aircraft was sent to the 'Skunk Works' for repair, it was rejected by the USAF upon its return to service for being all but impossible to fly correctly. Lockheed gave it to NASA, who adjusted the aircraft's flying controls, and it performed well for many years as an ER-2 research aircraft until given back to the USAF in 1996.

By 1990 the TR-1A's versatility in data transfer had become a reason for its survival as the 9th SRW began to shut down its SR-71 activity. Excessive expense and complexity in operating the Mach 3+ 'sleds' was condemned by the cost-cutters, led by the USAF Chief of Staff, Gen Larry D Welch. Also, the SR-71 lacked the TR-1's datalink capability, and Welch considered that the 'sled's' advantages compared with the TR-1A were 'marginal'. Loiter time capability and real-time data gathering became more important than speed and altitude.

In 1975 it was realised that adding a satellite antenna to the TR-1A would free the aircraft from its 250-mile orbits from the ground station to which it was data-linked. An antenna could allow the TR-1 to upload its data to a multi-channel Defense Systems Communications Satellite, which then passed it wherever it was needed. Using installation sketches done in 1975 by Lockheed designer Bob Anderson, TR-1 80-1071 was fitted with a 17-ft-long dorsal pod for the *Senior Span* project. It contained a 30-inch steerable parabolic antenna that could relay SIGINT while tracking a satellite as the aircraft flew its orbits, using the TR-1A's INS to provide accurate data on the aircraft's location.

A better, faster and less power-consuming uplink system for the *Span* housing known as *Senior Spur* was introduced in 1992, by which time the

'TR-1' title had been dropped and the aircraft became the U-2R once again. Its range of reconnaissance loads became so varied and frequently updated that, as Maj Randle commented, 'As far as combinations of mission equipment is concerned, it's incredible! It seems that the aircraft are sprouting new antennas every time I turn around'. While TR-1s took on most of the electronic reconnaissance duties, the U-2Rs were usually configured with cameras for what was by then known as IMINT (image intelligence).

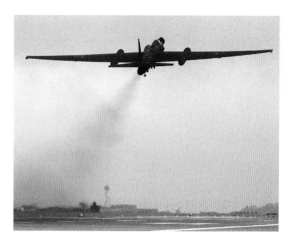

Climbing steeply away from the Alconbury runway, a TR-1A from the 95th FS/17th RW heads out on a training mission on 18 October 1989 (*USAF*)

There was a small aerodynamic price for having this large addition to the airframe, as Col Gaines noted;

'The *Span/Spur* antenna caused more drag and kept you from getting as much altitude, but not by a significant amount. Also, it added drag during the flare to landing, and maybe could cause you to lose speed a little faster and "drop it in", but, again, not by a significant amount. Neither of these modifications were ever installed in the two-seater, so the first time a pilot would fly them he was solo in a mission-loaded aircraft. The first time I ever saw a *Spur*-loaded aircraft was ferrying one from Sicily to Al Dhafra after "9/11". One of the other line pilots basically told me about the drag issue, and off I went and landed in the UAE [United Arab Emirates] with no problems.'

Another electronic breakthrough in the 1980s enabled the development of Itek's *Senior Year* Electro-Optic Reconnaissance System (SYERS). It used a 70-inch focal length LOROP camera mounted in a nose housing that could be rotated to allow a mirror system to 'look' left, right or down through a circular window. The large camera body in the nose would take images and then transmit them as electro-optical data to a ground station that operated in a similar way to the ASARS station.

SYERS obtained instantly available imagery at twice the range of the Type H camera. Put into production, it proved to be a valuable asset in Operation *Desert Shield* in 1990, with U-2Rs operating from OL-CH – Taif, Saudi Arabia. *Olympic Flare* missions were flown from 19 August, and *Senior Span* and SYERS missions began two days later. On 24 September Iraqi jets – a MiG-25 and a Mirage F1 – made a rare attempt to intercept a U-2R. Careful manoeuvring and use of defensive ECM caused them both to fall away and abandon the chase.

Further updates to the aircraft, details of which take the story beyond the scope of this volume, were first proposed in the late 1980s, since the TR-1 was the last aircraft in US service to use the J75 engine. Operational economies dictated the choice of a new engine then in current service use. The weight and performance penalties of the U-2R/TR-1 versions caused by the addition of ASARS, *Senior Span* and other systems also needed compensation by more thrust. The General Electric F-101-GE-29, which was soon to power the B-2A Spirit bomber, was chosen. It offered similar power to the J75. TR-1A 80-1090 was selected as the testbed, and it first flew in May 1989. Re-designated the F118-GE-101, the engine became the basis of the U-2S, which included other updates such as a one-piece windscreen. However, the new engine presented one difficulty, as Col Mason Gaines explained;

Veteran 68-10329 was the first U-2R in
August 1968. After conversion to
production standard in 1969, followed by
CIA and flight test service, the 9th SRW
took the aircraft over in 1981 and it had
been re-engined as a U-2S by May 1995.
Here, it has an ASARS nose in *Senior Spur*
configuration, including the dorsal antenna
structure known as the 'Big Top' (*USAF*)

'The J75 engine could be air-started multiple times after descending into thicker air, as it would windmill enough RPM to get a start. With the turbofan F118, you had one shot with the hydrozine bottle, and that was it. A turbofan does not windmill the compressor section.'

However, the new engine offered many advantages;

'You could take off with less gas, fly longer and land with more in reserve. The F118 was also lighter. You basically came back with minimum fuel all the time with the J75. The F118 was also FADEC [Full Authority Digital Engine Control] controlled, so you could literally pull the throttle to idle at 70,000 ft and it would reduce RPM about two to three per cent to about 95 per cent, then automatically reduce it further as you descended. With the J75, RPM had to be closely managed by the pilot, and it would flame out if reduced too much or too rapidly.'

The weight saving associated with the F118 amounted to around 1300 lbs, with a 16 per cent improvement in fuel consumption. Performance benefits were an extra 3500 ft altitude and 1220 miles in range. As a further weight saver, some areas of the flying surfaces and undercarriage doors were replaced with lighter composite material. By 1998, the whole U-2 fleet had been converted to U-2S configuration, giving the 'Dragon Lady' many more years of service life.

Considering that Kelly Johnson's original CL-282 concept proposed a fragile glider that would belly land on return from a mission, and possibly fly a few more sorties before withdrawal, for the programme to enter its 70th year in 2025 is an outstanding achievement. Indeed, the U-2 concept may well live on in the proposed unmanned TR-X successor.

APPENDICES

COLOUR PLATES COMMENTARY

1
U-2A 56-6708 of the 4080th SRW, Laughlin AFB, Texas, June 1957
Being an early J-57-powered U-2, this aircraft had smaller engine intakes and a clear lacquered natural metal finish. The latter's reflectivity gave rise to many reports of 'UFOs' at altitudes far above commercial aircraft. 56-6708 became a U-2C in March 1966, only to then crash near Barksdale AFB on 1 July 1967 after wing

failure due to excessive application of g-forces. Capt Samuel Swart successfully ejected.

2
U-2F 56-6680 of the 4080th SRW, Bien Hoa (OL-20), South Vietnam, October 1964
This was one of three U-2s (56-6680, -6703 and -6707) converted for ELINT missions with 'ram's horn' antennas above their rear

fuselages. The projections acted as small aerofoils, and 56-6680 became so notorious for the 'porpoising' motions in flight that they caused it was known as 'sick 80'. Moving one 'horn' fractionally helped. As a U-2E, it was the first such aircraft to be painted black overall. In 1975 56-6680 visited Britain for the ALSS project, having previously participated in the first Det A deployment in 1956 as NACA 187.

3
U-2C 56-6716 of the 100th SRW, RAF Wethersfield, Essex, May 1975
Originally a 'hard nose' HASP U-2A-1 operating from Plattsburgh AFB and Ezeiza, 56-6716 was taken out of storage in March 1962 and converted into a U-2C. More than a decade later, the aircraft participated in Exercise *Olympic Jump* during ALSS trials. The 'Sabre' grey paint scheme seen in this profile was applied to all five ALSS U-2Cs, since the presence of 'black spyplanes' on British territory would have been politically embarrassing.

4
WU-2A 56-6715 of the 4080th SRW, McCoy AFB, Florida, October 1962
Several U-2As were designated WU-2A, implying weather research, which they did perform occasionally. This example was principally a HASP aircraft, sampling atomic radiation from Puerto Rico, Argentina, Alaska and Australia in 1960 and Panama in 1963. For the Cuban Missile Crisis in October 1962, it was recalled and forward-based at McCoy AFB. Converted to U-2G configuration in early 1965, 56-6715 was lost on 26 April that same year in a crash at Edwards North Base that killed Det G pilot Eugene 'Buster' Edens.

5
U-2F 56-6676 of the 4080th SRW, McCoy AFB, Florida, October 1962
Originally used for C configuration camera tests, this aircraft was one of the CIA U-2Fs transferred to the USAF for surveillance over Cuba. It retained the CIA Sea Blue scheme, with the addition of white *U.S. AIR FORCE* titling, serial number and 'stars and bars' (also added to U-2F 56-6675), as there was no time to apply the USAF's light grey paint scheme. It has the 'sugar scoop' IR protection tail extension and dorsal fairing containing HF radio and System 9 ECM equipment. The aircraft was shot down over Cuba on 27 October 1962, killing Maj Rudy Anderson.

6
U-2C 56-6693 of Det B, Incirlik, Turkey, 1 May 1960
'Article 360' was the last of the CIA U-2A batch, delivered on 5 November 1956 and used for Det C's first overflight of the USSR on 8 June 1957. After test work until May 1959, it had been converted into a U-2C by August. Damaged in a forced landing at Fujisawai, Japan, the following month, it was repaired and issued to Det B at Incirlik. On 1 May 1960, the unmarked Sea Blue aircraft was shot down near Sverdlovsk during Operation *Grand Slam*, which had originated from Peshawar. Pilot Francis Gary Powers was captured.

7
U-2D 56-6953 of the 4080th SRW, Davis-Monthan AFB, Arizona 1965
SAC U-2s adopted a flat black scheme in 1965 instead of ADC Gray. This was one of the supplementary batch of U-2s built from spare

components and used for *Toy Soldier* and *Congo Maiden* missions in 1959–60. It was converted to U-2C configuration in 1966, stored and then used for training. Badly damaged in a 1972 accident at Davis-Monthan, it re-emerged as the first U-2CT trainer in 1973. After retirement in 1987, the aircraft was given to the Cold War Museum at Bodø, in Norway, where, once again, it became a U-2C.

8
U-2F 56-6692 of USAF Systems Command, Edwards AFB, California, 1972–74
A much-travelled U-2, this aircraft began service with the CIA's Det A in October 1956, before moving to SAC in December 1960 and then back to the CIA in 1962 as a U-2F. It flew Cuba missions in 1963 and flight-tested the U-2R configuration in 1965–67. USAF Systems Command took 56-6692 over in 1968, and in 1971 it became the sole Target Radiation Intensity Measurement testbed, with two rotating dorsal IR tracking sensors (as depicted here) to measure radiation levels of re-entry vehicles and missiles. The aircraft then reverted to U-2C specifications for the ALSS project, before being converted into a U-2CT.

9
U-2F 56-6682/N802X of Det G, Takhli RTAFB, Thailand, 1963
Overall black was replaced by the radar-absorbent 'black velvet' finish on CIA U-2s and a 'sugar scoop' was added to the tailpipe. N802X ('N' civilian registrations were exclusively used for CIA flights within the USA) flew with APQ-56 side-looking radar and participated in Project *Buckhorn* 'stealth' tests in 1958. After three years with the USAF's Air Research and Development Command, it reverted to CIA ownership in 1964 as a U-2H before modification into a U-2G the following year. From 1971 through to its retirement in 1989, the aircraft was used by NASA for research as N709A.

10
U-2C 56-6691/3512 of the 35th Squadron, RoCAF, Taoyuan AB, Taiwan, 1965
Finished in CIA Sea Blue, this U-2 was delivered to the Agency in October 1956, converted into a U-2C in 1959 and then transferred to the 'Black Cats' squadron. On a Project *Idealist* mission over the Baotau nuclear facility on 10 January 1965, 3512 was shot down by a 1st SAM Battalion Red Flag missile after the U-2C's ECM was defeated by counter-jamming. Maj 'Jack' Chang Li-Yi ejected and was captured.

11
U-2C 56-6952 of the 100th SRW, Davis-Monthan AFB, Arizona, 1969
Initially assigned to the 4080th SRW at Laughlin AFB in 1958, this aircraft flew *Toy Soldier* and *Congo Maiden* missions in 1959. Converted into a U-2C in 1966, it was used for training. The full-length dorsal fairing contained an aerial refuelling receptacle, HF radio and parts of the System 9 ECM suite. It was lost in a fatal accident at Davis-Monthan on 18 November 1971 when Capt John Cunney stalled while attempting a 'go-around' after a heavy landing.

12
U-2D 56-6721 of the Air Force Flight Test Center, Edwards AFB, California, 1976
Delivered to the 4080th SRW in October 1957, this aircraft, as a U-2A, made a belly landing at Cortez, in Colorado, in August 1959.

After repairs, 56-6721 remained at Edwards for test flying until 1978, the jet having been modified into a J57-engined U-2D (briefly designated U-2B) with a second observer's cockpit. It participated in testing of various IR sensor systems to detect incoming intercontinental missiles in Project *Smokey Joe*.

13
U-2R 68-10339, *Senior Lance* and EP-X trials, various locations, 1968–72

This U-2R first flew in October 1968 as N819X. It was initially used for trials, testing the *Senior Lance* (UPD-X) digital radar imagery and datalink equipment at Davis-Monthan, McCoy and Upper Heyford until 1972. 68-10339 then trialled imaging radars in an inflatable radome for the US Navy's EP-X project, before serving with the 100th SRW from early 1972 and the 9th SRW from 1976. It was lost on a training flight from Beale on 13 December 1993, killing pilot Capt Richard Schneider.

14
U-2A/D 56-6722 of the USAF Air Research and Development Command, Edwards AFB, early 1961

Used in Project *Smokey Joe* (hence the tail artwork) to test the 'Pickle Barrel' Baird-Atomic spectrometer, or radiometer, for detecting IR radiation from incoming ICBMs, 56-6722 had black upper surfaces forward of the wing trailing edge to prevent reflected sunlight from confusing the IR sensor. The fairing behind the sensor covered a communications antenna. The aircraft was retired in 1978 after a long test career that included trials of re-entry capsules for MIDAS satellite film. It has been on display in the USAF Museum at Wright-Patterson AFB, Ohio, for more than 40 years.

15
U-2G 56-6685/N315X of Det G, USS *Kitty Hawk* (CVA-63), NAS North Island, California, March–May 1964

A CIA U-2A from 1956, this aircraft became a U-2C in 1959, after which it was used by Lockheed and Det G for development flying through to 1963. For Project *Whale Tale* carrier trials by Bob Schumacher in 1964, N315X became a U-2G with 'black velvet' finish, a tailhook with fuselage reinforcements and fake *OFFICE OF NAVAL RESEARCH* markings. Subsequently flown by the RoCAF's 'Black Cats' squadron in 1965, the aircraft crashed into the sea off Taiwan on 22 October, possibly due to a faulty autopilot. Maj 'Pete' Wang Chen-Wen was killed.

16
U-2R 68-10329/3925 of Det H/35th Squadron, RoCAF, Taoyuan AB, Taiwan, 1970

U-2Rs with Type H cameras flew missions off the Chinese coast throughout 1970–71, surveying defence and transport sites and monitoring microwave communications. Two aircraft were usually based at Taoyuan with small RoCAF insignia, black velvet finish and fake serials.

17
U-2R 68-10331 of Det H/35th Squadron RoCAF, Taoyuan AB, Taiwan, 1971

This aircraft was one of just four of the original 12 U-2Rs to survive

for conversion into a U-2S in 1995. It was delivered to the CIA in 1968 as N800X, flying sampling missions in 1973 with the F-4 foil system. 68-10331 was passed to the 100th SRW in early 1975 and then on to the 9th SRW the following year, flying from Osan with Det 2 and the 5th RS on a rota patrolling the Demilitarized Zone. There, in the 1990s, it adopted the 35th Squadron's 'Black Cats' tail insignia – this aircraft has been one of the final two U-2Rs to leave Taoyuan after the 35th's flights ended in 1974.

18
U-2R 68-10340 of the 100th SRW, Bien Hoa AB, South Vietnam, 1969

Delivered as N820X in November 1968, 68-10340 was the last of the original 12 U-2Rs built by Lockheed. The 100th SRW received it in December, and by July 1969 the aircraft was flying from Bien Hoa over the Ho Chi Minh Trail in Laos and Cambodia. In July 1970 U-2R operations moved to U-Tapao. It crashed on 5 October 1980 at Osan, Capt Cleveland H Wallace surviving the accident.

19
U-2R 68-10329 of Det 4, 9th SRW, RAF Mildenhall, Suffolk, December 1979

This was the first U-2R, initially flown unpainted as N803X and then modified to production standard for the CIA in March 1969. 68-10329 was used in ongoing trials from 1974, including those for *Senior Spear*, before being re-issued to the 9th SRW. Converted into a U-2S, it returned to the 9th SRW in May 1995.

20
U-2CT 56-6692 of the 4029th SRTS/9th SRW, Beale AFB, California, 1980

As the second U-2CT for the 9th SRW, this aircraft was converted from a U-2C in 1976 (see Profile 8) and used to train pilots until December 1987. From February 1988 it served as a battle-damage repair training airframe at Alconbury, after which it was restored to U-2C configuration and delivered to the Imperial War Museum at Duxford, in Cambridgeshire, in 1992.

21
TR-1A 80-1082 of the 99th SRS/9th SRW, Beale AFB, California, 1989

This aircraft was delivered to the 9th SRW in November 1985 and was subsequently converted into a U-2S by January 1997. It has standard 'superpods'. The 9th SRW had to establish the 4029th Strategic Reconnaissance Training Squadron to train 'drivers' for the new variant. 80-1082 was lost at Al Dhafra, in the UAE, on 22 June 2005 after engine failure on final approach to land at the end of a mission over Afghanistan, killing the unnamed pilot.

22
U-2R 68-10336 of the Lockheed Flight Test Center, Palmdale, California, 1982

First flown on 20 August 1968 as N816X, this U-2R served with the 100th SRW from August 1968 until transferred to the 9th SRW in 1976. By 1981 it had returned to Lockheed at Palmdale, where it was converted into a U-2S and flown by Det 2 of the Combined Test Force with an extended nose for the TR-1A/ASARS programme.

INDEX